EXTRAORDINARY RESOLVE

SIX MONTHS FOR THE REST OF MY LIFE

BOB YOUNGS

with Michele Stanek

EXTRAORDINARY RESOLVE

SIX MONTHS FOR THE REST OF MY LIFE

Editing and book composition by E. Pirrung.

This book is dedicated to anyone whose life has been touched by cancer.

To all the family members and friends—be supportive. More importantly, just be there for your loved ones. It truly does make a difference.

To all the survivors—congratulations and pass on what you have been through to those who are there now.

To all the current patients—fight the good fight and never, ever give up hope. You can make it through this.

— Bob Youngs

Contents

Preface

ALWYN COSGROVE

MY ENTIRE YOUTH, teenage years, and early twenties were spent wanting to be a great fighter. I entered the world of combat sports in my early teens and soon became obsessed with it.

I fought everything. Mixed martial arts didn't exist then. If it did, that's surely where I would have gone. Instead, I fought in tae kwon do events, open martial arts tournaments, kickboxing, you name it. I traveled the United Kingdom, Europe, and eventually the world trying to prove I was a great fighter. I wanted to be—as Mike Tyson once eloquently put it—"the baldest mother***err on the planet."

I won seven national titles over five different weight classes. I suppose my career fizzled out shortly after winning the California state tae kwon do championship in 2000. But my mindset of wanting to show the world how great a fighter I was never went away...

As they say, be careful what you wish for.

Every religion in the world has some sort of saying along the lines of "Ask and ye shall receive." Modern "life coaches" refer to the "law of attraction."

In 2004, I was about to become the greatest fighter I could ever imagine. However, as Mr. Miyagi once said to Daniel-san in the movie *Karate Kid*: "This is not tournament. This is for real!"

From 2004 to 2006, I fought stage IV cancer. There isn't any stage V cancer. Stage V is death.

I won that fight. Today as I write this, in May 2010, I have been in remission for four years after rounds and rounds of chemotherapy and a bone marrow and stem cell transplant. I am a cancer survivor.

And I no longer want to prove how hard I can fight.

In 2009, my friend Dave Tate sent me an email about a fellow Team EliteFTS member by the name of Bob Youngs, who had been diagnosed with leukemia. Dave didn't ask me to do anything, as I'd never met Bob.

But that's not how it works. Your job as a cancer survivor is to be a coach and a confidant, the guy who gives a slap or a shoulder to cry on, the guy who gives whatever is needed to those about to start the journey. Because once you hear the words "you have cancer," your world is never the same again, and only other people who have been told the same thing can even come close to understanding.

I reached out to Bob to tell him that I was on his team. And I reached out to Michele, Bob's fiancée, to let her know that she was about to be part of a fight she didn't even know was coming.

Welcome to the club that you never wanted to join. And can't wait to leave. Cancer may be the biggest one-on-one fight you'll ever face, but it's a 100 percent team sport. And I was on their team whether they liked it or not.

There's a weird bond between people who have faced cancer that I just can't explain. I've still never met Bob, but I knew every emotion, negative thought, and fear that was running through his head. Then. Now. And probably in the future.

I emailed Bob:

> *"A man fell into a hole and couldn't get out. A doctor walked by, and the man yelled up, "Can you help me? I can't get out!" The doctor wrote a prescription, threw it down into the hole, and walked away.*
>
> *A priest walked by, and the man yelled up, "Help! I've fallen into a hole and can't get out."*
>
> *The priest wrote a prayer on a piece of paper, threw it down to the man, and walked on.*

> *Soon the man's friend walked by. "Hey, friend! I've fallen into this hole and can't get out. Can you help me?"*
>
> *The friend said, "Sure," and jumped into the hole with his friend.*
>
> *The man said, "Are you crazy? Now we're both stuck in this hole!"*
>
> *But his friend said, "No, see. I've been in this hole before, and I know how to get out."*

Six months of the toughest fighting you can imagine. Bob Youngs has joined the new club—the cancer survivors. Still not a club you really want to belong to but a club that's a lot better than the last club. And it's a club you never want to leave.

Bob knew he was strong, but he didn't know how strong he was. This had nothing to do with a three-lift total and everything to do with the man he was inside.

I joked with Michele—Bob is so strong he beat cancer while he was unconscious! Most of us had to at least stay awake!

I'm honored to write this foreword and to have been in Team Bob Youngs' corner as he went head to head with his own mortality. And I'm proud that we're both on the same team now.

I'll leave you with verses from a couple of songs that say more than I ever could:

It's a blur since they told me about it
How the darkness had taken its toll.
And they cut into my skin and they cut into my body,
but they will never get a piece of my soul.
And now I'm still learning the lesson
to awake when I hear the call.
And if you ask me why I am still running,
I'll tell you I run for us all.

I run for hope.
I run to feel.
I run for the truth
For all that am real.
I run for your mother, your sister, your wife.
I run for you and me, my friend.
I run for life.

— Melissa Etheridge

My pride is left for dead, as my world gets shaken.
The thoughts inside my head
so hard to control.
I am staring down the unknown,
but one thing is certain.
You could break my body,
but you will never break my soul.

And they say the road to heaven, it might lead us back through hell,
but we're holding on for more than stories to tell.

Maybe tonight, maybe tomorrow,
we will win this fight and bury this sorrow.
We're so alive, still holding on, not ready to die, so we LIVE STRONG.

— *Wide-awake*

Bob, I look forward to meeting you in person some day soon. But I already know you.

— Alwyn Cosgrove
Two-time cancer survivor
Team Bob Youngs' member

P.S. FUCK cancer.

Preface

DAVE TATE

"ARE YOU BROTHERS?"

Bob and I looked at each other and at the same time replied, "Oh, hell no." This isn't an unusual question to be asked when two guys, both over 275 lbs with bald heads and goatees, are sitting at Bob Evans. Next to "How much can you bench press," this question ranks in the top five questions meatheads get asked—maybe the first when we travel in pairs.

This was my last meal before the 1998 IPA Worlds, and Bob was in charge of me. Yes, that's a correct statement. Todd Brock and Bob had decided the week before that it would be in my best interests if one of them stayed with me from the time we got to the meet site until the meet was over. They knew from past experience that I was my own worst enemy when it came to meet time. This wasn't due to nerves, jitters, fear, or any other typical pre-meet issue but more to my overarousal. I had a tendency during meets to completely turn off who I was and become another person. They had tried in the past to control this while I was in the meet, but it never worked. This time their game plan was different. They wanted to fix the problem before it ever happened.

At the time, I had no idea what was going on and couldn't figure out why they wouldn't leave me alone. By the time this lunch came around, I was pretty sick of both of them. So when the waitress asked if Bob was my brother, I was about ready to kill him. I'm sure he felt the same way about me.

The meet came and went. Looking back on over 100 meets that I've competed in, this was the best meet of my life by the books and by the memories. This is the one meet I will never forget. Everything went right. I was in 100 percent control. We had a great time, and I broke personal records across the board. During that meet, I discovered that handlers do more than just lift bars out and call squat depth. This is a lesson that continues with me every year.

One year after this meet, I started the company Elite Fitness Systems. One of the very first things I did was write a list of values. I wanted to use these values to build the company and my life. I knew this venture wouldn't mean anything if I didn't have someone on the outside looking in, someone to make sure I lived up to my own standards and expectations, someone who would have the will and fortitude to tell me if I was falling off track, and someone I would be willing to listen to.

I knew many people who wouldn't have had any problem telling me the truth, but I could only trust one person who would and could be brutally honest if needed. This wasn't just about me. I had a family to think about and a future staff whose lives would be affected by my actions. I asked Bob to be this person, and he agreed with a statement that I will never forget. He said, "This is great, and I'd be happy to do this. Now, are you willing to use these values as your guiding values, and do you really understand what this means?"

At this point, I knew I had the right man for the job. He understood that these weren't rules but guiding values to help lead me in the direction I wanted to go. He also understood that I would make mistakes, but he wanted me to know that these values would help pull me back in line. This discussion with Bob wasn't a long one. I've never needed to have long conversations with Bob. It's hard to explain, but we know each other and can get a grasp of what's going on with just a few questions. I don't know. Maybe we have some weird type of voodoo connection, but it works. It works in ways that have had major impacts on my life.

Years later, Bob moved back to Florida. We emailed and spoke from time to time. We saw each other on occasion, but I always knew he was there. Sometimes I received an email from him asking simple questions about my family, training, business, or my kids, and each time he sent these questions, I had something going on that was working against my values. It was like he sensed this, and his email was a reminder to me to get my priorities straight. To this day, I can't tell you how he knew, but he always did.

During what I would describe as the worst time of my life, Bob was there in a way no one else was. He was there with brutal honesty.

There aren't any words to describe the impact this had on me other than I spent the next six hours sitting on a bench looking at the "reality" of my life, not the fantasy everyone else tells you, not the "everything happens for a reason" statement, not the "you will be OK" crap. No, I was just smacked in the face with the truth of my situation by someone who I trusted to be honest with me. To say this reality changed my life is an understatement. Actually, it didn't change my life at all. We are who we are, but it made me better understand who I am and how I create the situations and circumstances around me.

Over a year ago, my wife and I went on a cruise vacation with Bob and his fiancée Michele. We had been looking forward to this trip for some time and it was great to meet up with friends, especially on vacation. Unfortunately, Bob was sick most of the time. It was very easy to tell he was ill because he looked horrible, but he still managed to go on a few excursions, meet for dinner, and attend a few other activities. I never heard him complain once, and he wanted to make sure Michele and the rest of us were still having a good time. The day after we docked Bob checked into the hospital, and my wife and I caught our flight back home. A couple days later, I was told that Bob had leukemia and was staying in the hospital. He needed to undergo chemotherapy. You'll read about his fight throughout the pages of this book.

After hearing the news, I didn't know what to think. Like everyone else, I was stunned. I didn't know what to say or do, but I did know someone who would know what to say. After hearing the news, my very first call was to my friend Alwyn Cosgrove. Alwyn knew this battle and knew it well. I hoped he would call and speak to Bob and Michele and just let them know what they were in for. Little did I know how big of a role and how much of a help Alwyn would be.

Many days passed and very few of those days were good. It seemed one thing led to another, and the situation just got worse and worse. Then I got a call informing me that the priest had been called in and there was a very good chance Bob wouldn't make it through the day. All I remember about that conversation is saying, "If he isn't dead, don't count him out. There will be time to mourn if needed." However, at that moment, we needed to stay positive and only think that Bob was one of the one percent who makes it.

I hate percentages because of the negativity they imply. Who is to say you aren't that one percent? Why do people always assume you're in the percentage that's bad? Bob was surrounded by people who put him in that one percent category so he pulled through. Why? None of us know. Was it our positive thoughts, some miracle, chance, luck, the law of attraction? I'm not sure. What I do know is our positive thoughts and prayers certainly didn't hurt while our negativity would have weakened his entire support network. It was only a year earlier that Bob reinforced this to me, and there wasn't any way I was going to forget it then.

After Bob was sent to the Cleveland Clinic, I made my first visit to see him. I was told beforehand that he didn't look good. He had lost a ton of weight and had tubes all over him. None of this mattered to me. I was there to work and help out in any way I could. Before walking into the room, I had to don a blue plastic gown, gloves, and a mask. When I walked in, Bob didn't look anything like what I had been told. He looked worse! Regardless, I saw this as ground zero, and the goal was to get a tiny bit better, a little stronger, and a tiny bit more positive each day. The healing, the medicines, and the treatments weren't my deal. I didn't know anything about that. What I did know was what it felt like to have someone really care when you're in a time of need, someone willing to tell you the truth when others may shy away, and someone who didn't really care about the drama or pain but just the person inside. Once again, it was the person lying in that bed who reinforced these values for me.

A few hours went by. A nurse walked in and asked, "Are you brothers?"

We both replied, "Yes!"

This book will show you the true nature of strength, the strength of being a powerlifter, the strength of fighting cancer, and the strength of being a survivor. Bob is a man of character and strength, and I'm proud to tell anyone that he is my brother.

Introduction

BOB YOUNGS

I'M GOING TO DIE. That's all I could think about. The doctor had just given me the news that I had leukemia. After she walked out, I cried. I cried like I had never cried before. I was pissed off at everyone and everything. I was mad at God, Satan, my doctors, and even the guy snoring in the bed next to me. I was also sad. How could this happen to me? Why me? What would my son do without me?

The thing that angered and scared me the most was I wouldn't be able to see my son grow up. I figured the rest of my family and friends would be OK without me. They would move on and hopefully speak of me kindly on occasion when they remembered me. But my son Christopher? He needed me. How could this happen?

I spent the first day asking myself all these kinds of questions. I've talked to many cancer patients, and everyone seems to do the same thing when they're told they have cancer. I still haven't figured out why me. Bad stuff happens to good people, and there isn't any explanation for it. I have learned that all you can do is worry about what you can control.

The next day I woke up and decided I was going to live. I wouldn't give up and I wouldn't stop fighting. I would do whatever I needed to do and I would do it with all of my being. My son wasn't going to grow up without a father and my family and friends weren't going to lose me.

This is the story of my six-month fight with leukemia. Obviously, you wouldn't be reading this if I had lost that fight. My journey was full of many life-threatening twists and turns. My fiancée, Michele Stanek, kept a blog for our friends and family to follow along and receive updates. I have included her blog because it gives me a basis to write about what I was feeling and thinking. My comments on Michele's blog are italicized.

The Journey

WEDNESDAY, JUNE 24, 2009

First entry

Dear Family and Friends,

This is the first entry of my blog to keep everyone up to date on Bob and how he's doing. I guess I should start from the beginning and let everyone know what has happened so far.

As most of you know, Bob and I went with his friends, Dave and Traci, on vacation to celebrate his 39th birthday this past week. A few days before the trip, Bob was complaining of stomach pain. I wasn't feeling well myself, so we thought we had both picked up a bug of some sort. We started on vacation and I was feeling better, but Bob was feeling much worse. So for the first two days of the trip, Bob stayed in the room.

Bob was actually feeling better over the next few days, so much so that he went scuba diving with me in Honduras and climbed the Mayan ruins with Dave, Traci, and me in Belize. Unfortunately, he started to feel worse again. When our vacation ended that Sunday (on Father's Day), I persuaded Bob to go to the walk-in clinic near our house to see a doctor because he hurt all over. The doctor had concerns about Bob's stomach being so tender and did a test to determine if he was bleeding internally. It came back positive, and I rushed Bob to Bethesda Memorial Hospital in Boynton Beach, Florida.

Thank God the emergency room people were very quick to react. They told me they were surprised Bob was still walking with all the blood he had lost. They had to drain blood from his stomach and immediately started a blood transfusion. He needed six pints of blood initially. Just to give you an idea of how much he lost the average person has 8–12 pints of blood in his entire body.

We spent the night in the emergency room, and on Monday morning, they transferred Bob to the intensive care unit (ICU). They needed to get him stable before they could perform the remaining colonoscopy and upper gastrointestinal (GI) endoscopy on Tuesday. In the meanwhile, they decided to perform a million tests to try to figure out where he was losing blood from (he needed an additional three pints of blood Monday night). He was tested for everything from swine flu to bacterial infections. They decided to include a bone marrow aspiration as well because they found enlarged lymph nodes in his stomach. The colonoscopy was normal, and the upper GI showed a few ulcers. His blood was starting to maintain itself on Tuesday night so we hoped for the best, and I went to work Wednesday morning. Unfortunately, while I was at work, the oncologist came by the ICU and informed Bob of the bad news. Preliminary test results from the bone marrow aspiration showed he has leukemia—acute myeloid leukemia to be exact. Believe it or not, this is the exact same cancer his mom had. So Wednesday morning they moved Bob to the cancer center at the hospital and he'll start chemotherapy first thing in the morning. I've been getting lots of emails from people wanting to visit Bob. Unfortunately, right now his immune system is pretty much shot to hell due to the blood loss, so he is living in a sterile environment with masks and everything. Chemotherapy starts tomorrow and lasts for seven days, so I'll be writing more soon.

I'd just like to say thank you from the bottom of my heart for all the support, love, and prayers everyone has given Bob. It really means a lot to him. I'm especially grateful to Dave, Jim, and Alwyn from EliteFTS.com, all his powerlifting buddies, his co-workers, and all of our family and friends. He won't be able to check his email much starting tomorrow, so we've decided that I'm going to read him all the comments people make here on the blog for him. So keep the comments and support coming!

— Michele

For the purpose of this book, my oncologist will be called "the Dr." She was great through the whole thing. When she told me I had leukemia, I think it hurt her as much as it did me. The three days spent in the hospital were a blur when I got the news. It was like being smacked by a 2 X 4. I asked if I could go home for a day because I wanted to see my son. The Dr. said no because she needed to start the treatment right away. I spent the first day being mad at the world and asking why me?

I was also so damn scared. I feared my life was over. The statistics for me living beyond five years were less than fifty percent. If I did live through chemo, what would my life be like? How would I make a living? How would I play with my son? Would life ever be "normal" again?

The next day I decided I wanted to live. I decided I would do whatever I needed to do, and I was going to be OK. I tried as best I could to block out the thought of dying. Don't get me wrong—there were times the thought of death crept into my mind. But I had to think of living. It was on that second day that I decided my only option was to live.

THURSDAY, JUNE 25, 2009

Day one of chemotherapy

Dear Family and Friends,

Today Bob began his first day of "induction chemotherapy." I'm not sure how detailed everyone wants me to be, so I'll give the details just for this first entry. I know many people want to look this stuff up, so here it goes.

Bob will be taking a seven-day course of the drug Cytarabine, and on the last three days, they will add Idarubicin to the mix. Per his doctor, this is used to wipe out the bad cells from his bone marrow. The main side effect, aside from nausea, will be a risk of infection and blood loss due to not having an immune system. For this reason and the fact that his platelets are so low due to the prior internal bleeding, they're taking "neutropenic precautions" with Bob, who means he isn't allowed any flowers in the room, everyone must wear a mask and wash their hands before they see him, and he can't have any fresh fruit, veggies, or tap water. Right now, only immediate family can visit due to his compromised immune system. Bob is also being given Zofran to combat any potential nausea.

On the 14th day after chemotherapy begins, they will repeat the bone marrow biopsy to determine the effectiveness of the chemo. On the 30th day, they will begin "consolidation chemotherapy," which is an even higher dose of the Cytarabine and lasts for three days. They will keep repeating the chemotherapy cycle 3–4 times. After this and depending on how many of the cancer cells were eradicated, the next step is a possible stem cell or bone marrow transplant. We don't know about this part yet.

Unfortunately, we're still waiting for the results of the final cancer cytogenetic testing. We don't know what subtype of leukemia Bob has, which would help the doctors determine how strong it is. We hope to have these results by Monday.

On a more positive note, Bob is doing very well on his first day. He ate dinner and is just minimally nauseous. He says hello to everyone and is excited to watch *Burn Notice* tonight. (He wanted me to say this!)

Finally, I would like to especially thank my friend Rana today. She will be running a 5K in Hyde Park, London, on July 19th to raise money for cancer research. She is dedicating her run to Bob. Also, many thanks to everyone who has made donations on this site. Thanks again for all the texts, phone calls, emails, and comments as well. I'm telling Bob about each and every one of them. Thanks again for everything and I'll keep you posted.

— Michele

The way that Michele writes about it you would think chemotherapy isn't too bad. Just some IV drugs and a little upset stomach. My very good friend, Alwyn Cosgrove, is also a cancer survivor and has been through over twenty rounds of chemo. I barely made it through five. My mother walked out of chemo in the middle of round five. So I have no idea how in the hell Alwyn did that many. Alwyn is one of the US's most famous fitness trainers (www.alwyncosgrove.com). He was also a tae kwon do international champion. So Alwyn is a bad dude. But going through that many rounds of chemo impresses me more than his ability in martial arts.

Alwyn had the best description of chemo that I've come across yet. He said chemo is like the worst hangover of your life. You know that hangover when you get up and pray to God that if you live through the day you'll never drink again? That's chemo. Little did I know I had six months ahead of me of feeling liked that?

But I was up for it. I had spent most of my youth and into my college years as an athlete. I played football, hockey, and baseball in high school. I played three years of college football before tearing my knee up and then two years of college hockey after that. I then got into powerlifting and spent the majority of my adult life chasing bigger lifts. I had always been able to just play my way through pain. So chemo became a game of pain for me. I'd rather take the pain than have someone else in my family take it. I got the pain I knew was coming. I got it in spades.

I remember staring at the chemo bag for hours. Would this magic potion cure me or kill me? The nurse who administered it had to wear heavy gloves just to touch the bag in case it somehow leaked. A second nurse had to watch the first nurse put the bag in. They tried not to look at me, and they had a businesslike attitude during the whole process. But all I could think about was that this was beyond anything I had ever confronted. Was I really up for it? I had so much time to think and most of it was negative. I searched for the positives and struggled to find them. What did I really have to be positive about?

FRIDAY, JUNE 26, 2009

Day two of chemotherapy

Dear Family and Friends,

Today is day two of chemotherapy, and so far things aren't as good as yesterday, but they aren't horrible either. Bob is a little more nauseous, and I didn't help things by mopping his floor with antibacterial wipes. (I was trying to get his room as sterile as possible so he won't catch anything.) I'll know not to do that again...

I went to Bob's office this morning to pick up some of his personal items (photos, his glasses). Everyone there was fantastic, and it was great to see everyone again. Also, I dropped off the paperwork to put Bob on short-term disability.

Other than that, not much new to report. My mom and Bob's mom stopped by this afternoon to visit him and drop off some candy and cookies (candy to bribe the nurses and cookies for Bob). They also brought some much needed Gatorade. That's about it. Bob said he was a little disappointed with *Burn Notice* last night. He didn't think it was as good as usual. He is also in the process of trying to find out if he gets TBS so he can watch baseball during the day. Finally, for all the powerlifters out there, you'd be happy to know that Bob is maintaining a daily workout—he walks four times a day around the wing!

He wanted me to give everyone a huge thank you for the comments you've been posting.

— Michele

My mom was great during this whole ordeal. My mother is a breast cancer and leukemia survivor, so she was best prepared to help. When people visit, they don't know what to say. My mom, having been through this, always knew just what to say. She also knew how to bribe the nurses with candy, so the nurses always liked taking care of me because we had food for them.

Michele's mom, Mary, is one of those people always described by others as one of the nicest people you'll ever meet. Mary is also a breast cancer survivor, so she could relate as well. I really enjoyed her company. It was great to talk to my two moms, but I started to feel guilty. I felt really bad about Michele having to go through this. Being the idiot I can be at times, I told her to leave me. She didn't need this and it wasn't her fight. I told her to move on and that she would find someone who made her happy. Who would want to be with someone who statistically was going to die in the next five years?

Well she put me in my place rather quickly and was pissed off that I would even suggest something like that. To burn off her anger, she decided to clean the room. I was already very nauseous, and she used antibacterial wipes. The smell made me want to puke like you couldn't imagine. Needless to say, I learned my lesson. Michele proved to be stronger than I ever could've known. Without her by my side, I'd be dead. There isn't any doubt in my mind. How do you pay someone back for that?

I remember going for one of my walks around the oncology ward. You can't help but to look in the rooms. Everyone looked miserable. Everywhere I looked I saw sick people, and people were dying in my mind. I could hear moaning coming from some of the rooms. That wouldn't be me, would it? Would that be my life or my death?

SATURDAY, JUNE 27, 2009

Day three of chemotherapy

Dear Family and Friends,

Today is day three of chemotherapy, and I asked Bob to tell me how he's feeling. He said "very tired." He spent the majority of the afternoon in bed and didn't have the energy to walk. His feet are very swollen with edema due to all the fluids from the chemo, so he might try walking tomorrow.

Christopher visited today. He showed us the flag football trophy he received because today was his final game. Bob had been Christopher's coach up until last weekend. Other than that, Bob's been watching the Red Sox game on television. He wanted me to say hello to everyone as well.

I'll post more tomorrow.

— Michele

I was feeling sorry for myself. My dad came in, and in his own way, he reminded me that it wasn't time to feel sorry for myself. He said, "It's time to fight." Not much of a statement on the surface, but it meant a lot coming from him. After he left, I sent this email to my close friends and family:

> *Hi everyone,*
> *I'll try and be brief, but I wanted to let you know how things were going and where I stand. As some of you know, my father is a former Navy SEAL, and when I grew up, he taught me how to fight. The first lesson he taught me was there aren't any fair fights. You just fight to win. The one standing in the end wins.*

My dad played a huge role in my chemotherapy and recovery. He visited almost every day. Many of those days we didn't exchange more than a couple words. I think just knowing that he was standing next to me during my fight was what really mattered to me. Even at 67, there wasn't anyone I'd rather have next to me in a fight than my dad. Sometimes it's the unspoken words that carry so much weight.

This was the first time my son, Christopher Thomas Youngs, had come to see me since I went into the hospital. I want to make it clear that my son isn't any better than anyone else's child. The only difference is that he's my son. That makes him the most important person in my life. He proved to be brave well beyond his six years of age. Can you imagine walking in to see your father in a hospital bed with tubes going in every direction? He didn't flinch. It took everything I had not to break down and cry in front of him, but I knew I couldn't do that. I had to put on the strong front and show no doubt. What choice did I have?

When he left, I broke down. I cried like you wouldn't believe. If possible, my decision to live was even more cemented in my mind. As you will see throughout this book, it's the little things that matter when you go through chemo. A hand squeeze from Michele, the nod of my dad's head, the smile on Christopher's face. Those are the things that carried me through.

SUNDAY, JUNE 28, 2009

Day four of chemotherapy

Dear Family and Friends,

Day four of chemo isn't going as well as yesterday. Bob spent almost all day in bed. He watched the Red Sox lose, and he's feeling even more nauseous than on day three. Christopher visited again and showed us his toys, and we played on the computer.

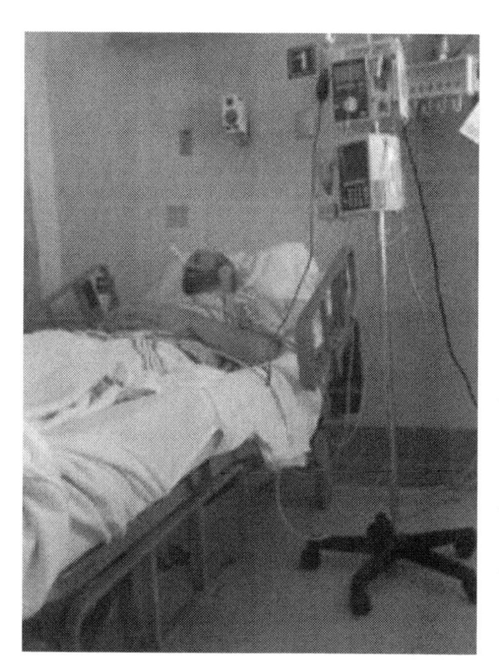

A special thank you to Kim Russo, who posted a comment on day three and sent us a link to her blog. There are other people here locally in south Florida who are going through the same kind of leukemia, and Bob isn't alone. When he's feeling up to it, I'll have him read Kim's blog.

— Michele

As you can probably tell by now, I'm a huge Red Sox fan. I grew up in Connecticut sitting in front of the television watching Red Sox games. More than anything else, I appreciate the game itself.

I just love to watch baseball. I got to watch a lot of baseball over the next couple of months. You see, when you're stuck in the hospital, you don't have much entertainment. It's pretty much television. I was too tired and sick to walk across the room to use my laptop. So it was the television and me. I look back now and certain shows remind me of being in the hospital. Whenever I see Cash Cab, *I feel like I am back in my hospital bed. I also think I saw every episode of* CSI *and* NCIS *ever made.*

Once again, I felt like crap. I couldn't eat. The thought of food made me feel like I was going to puke. I could barely roll over in my bed. My body just hurt. I mean from the top of my head to the bottom of my feet pain. Pain like I had never known before. But in walked my son. I often call him by his initials "CT." What did I do? I sat my ass up and put on my brave face. I said, "Hey CT. How are you?" He needed to know that his dad was OK. There wasn't any other option.

Michele had started this blog and it took on a life of its own. I can't tell you how many people were following, but the amount of daily hits to the blog shocked me. So many of my friends in the powerlifting community were following and my family was following as well. Somehow it grew. Word spread, especially once things turned for the worse, but I'm getting ahead of myself.

Remember, it's the little things. Kim took the time to write to me. She had her own issues, but she took time out of her day to write to me, someone she had never even met. Over the next six months, I was astonished by the kindness of total strangers and friends alike. Every time someone took the time to show me their support, it added to my resolve. I'm still amazed at the kindness of people. I still wonder what compelled people to reach out and offer help.

This was the first time I had thought of the people who made it through, the survivors, those who met this life-threatening disease and won the fight. Did I really have it in me? I walked the ward again. I saw rooms with visitors and crying people everywhere, some just having conversations in their rooms. The nurses, going about their work, nodded at me and smiled. Were they smiling because they thought I could make it or because they thought I was a goner? So many sick people in one place and too much time to think. I had to stop thinking. It was going to kill me. "Stay positive," I told myself. That would be so hard over the next six months.

MONDAY, JUNE 29, 2009

Day five of chemotherapy

Dear Family and Friends,

Unfortunately, as expected, day five is another day of nausea and weakness. Bob hasn't been able to walk the wing in a few days because he's been so tired. This morning they took some blood. They were trying to be proactive and figure out Bob's type in case he ever needed a stem cell transplant. However, the doctor realized that it's super expensive and they would need to do it over again at the Dana Farber Cancer Center in Boston anyway. So they basically drew his blood for nothing. Now he may need to get a blood transfusion tomorrow. We have to wait and see.

Speaking of Dana Farber, I started the paperwork to get Bob registered there today. Now all I have to do is get Bethesda to fax Bob's medical records to Boston for them to review. The people in Boston were very nice, and it looks like Bob's doctor up there will be the one his mom saw when she had leukemia. (I asked them and they said no problem.)

That's all that is going on here. Special thanks to Alwyn for the email he sent. Bob said he's going to watch *Secrets of the Founding Fathers* on the History Channel tonight. Thanks for all the thoughts and prayers.

— Michele

Michele is the absolute best patient advocate I could ever have asked for. That will become even more obvious soon. She was always trying to stay one step ahead in the process. I didn't really think a transplant would be needed. I don't know why, but in the back of my mind, I knew I was either going to die during chemo or be cured after. I have no idea why I thought this because it makes little sense, but I just didn't look at planning for a transplant as a big issue. Maybe it's because I had all I could handle on my plate?

I think I need to add more about Alwyn. I've never met Alwyn in person. He's a friend of my good friend, Dave Tate. Dave, who will play a big part in this story too, introduced us.

Alwyn sent me an email on this day:

> *"A man fell into a hole and couldn't get out. A doctor walked by, and the man yelled up, "Can you help me? I can't get out!" The doctor wrote a prescription, threw it down into the hole, and walked away.*
>
> *A priest walked by, and the man yelled up, "Help! I've fallen into a hole and can't get out." The priest wrote a prayer on a piece of paper, threw it down to the man, and walked on.*
>
> *Soon the man's friend walked by. "Hey, friend! I've fallen into this hole and can't get out. Can you help me?"*

The friend said, "Sure," and jumped into the hole with his friend.

The man said, "Are you crazy? Now we're both stuck in this hole!"

But his friend said, "No, see. I've been in this hole before, and I know how to get out."

Another day closer...

—AC

Alwyn jumped right in the hole with me. A man I had never met would help save my life. Alwyn became Michele's confidant during this whole ordeal. You see the hardest part of chemo and cancer is you have no idea what to expect. The fear of the unknown can be maddening. Alwyn and Michele were soon speaking almost daily.

TUESDAY, JUNE 30, 2009

Lots of news for Bob Youngs and day six of chemotherapy

Dear Family and Friends,

Lots of news today—some good and some not so well. For the good news, Bob and I are engaged! That really caught me off guard, and I never in a million years thought I would be proposed to in a hospital! Of course, I accepted. Apparently, he asked my dad for his permission while my dad was visiting him this morning.

Now for the not so good news—Bob's had a pretty rough day today. By far the worst day yet. He's in a severe amount of pain and really didn't have the energy to even sit in the chair. His pulse is also high. He's laying in bed and it's at 152 beats per minute. They just did some imaging of his stomach to make sure everything is OK. Earlier this morning, they had to give him another blood transfusion as well. For the first time, Bob asked me to spend the night in the hospital tonight just to keep an eye on him.

Thanks again for all the prayers and keep the comments and emails coming.

— Michele

Michele's parents came to visit, and I asked her dad, Dan, for his permission to marry Michele. I figured he couldn't say no to a guy stuck in a hospital bed, right? Luckily for me, he said yes. So when Michele came in that night I asked her to marry me. I was so weak I couldn't even stand. Forget about kneeling to propose. But she said yes. One more big reason for me to fight.

The pain, oh the pain. Chemo for me was about getting through the pain. A word of advice to all potential chemo patients or anyone with someone who is going through chemo—take all the pain medicines they'll give you. I'm sure any doctor reading that just cringed. But there isn't any need to suffer. I took all of my pain medicines and couldn't imagine doing it any other way. They don't fix everything, but they do help. I was getting Dilaudid every couple of hours. It made me feel better for about an hour and a half or so.

This day was the beginning of the really bad part. Little did I know, the fight was really about to begin soon. You think you're up for the fight, but you're always wondering, how will this end? It was maddening for me to not have control of my life. My life was in the hands of the doctors, and all I could do was fight. The loss of control was so difficult for me to deal with. My life was turning into a schedule of nurses' visits, doctors' visits, and tests. I had no control over any of it.

WEDNESDAY, JULY 1, 2009

Last night of chemo treatment

Dear Family and Friends,

Tonight is Bob's last bag of chemo. He's had a really rough day. Last night, he had a fever of 103° F, and they packed him with ice. It pretty much stayed the same throughout the night. His fever went down this morning to 101° F. The doctor told me she thought he might have an infection due to the effects of the chemo and his low blood counts, so they gave him broad spectrum antibiotics as well as a platelet transfusion. This afternoon his fever went back up to 103° F, and they had to pack him with ice again. He hasn't left the bed and hasn't been able to eat since a day and a half ago. The nutritionist is giving him Ensure, but he isn't keen on drinking it due to the nausea.

A special thanks to the people who are following Bob from Alwyn's blog. That's very kind of you. In addition, a super huge 'thank you' to everyone for all the congratulations about the engagement last night! I have recent photos of Bob and me from our trip ten days ago, and when I get home, I'll try to post some. It's pretty crazy what a difference ten days can make.

— Michele

Imagine burning up and laying there with ice packs all over your body. That was me. I was burning up and freezing all at the same time. I was shivering and sweating. This was when it really hit me that this was going to be harder than I had imagined. I couldn't eat. I felt like I was going to puke every second of the day. Imagine being seasick and having food poisoning at the same time. That's how my stomach felt.

Today I started my love-hate relationship with hospital personnel. I had many great nurses and a few not so great nurses. I had some great doctors and a couple of not so great doctors. I was lucky that the Dr. was my main doctor and I couldn't have asked for a better doctor in the world. The nutritionist was trying to demand that I eat or drink Ensure. I was fighting back vomit and she wanted to pour Ensure down my throat. Don't you think I would've eaten or drank if I could? Over the next six months, I was amazed how doctors thought that if they demanded something from me, I would just do it.

THURSDAY, JULY 2, 2009

More fevers, more blood, and pretty good news

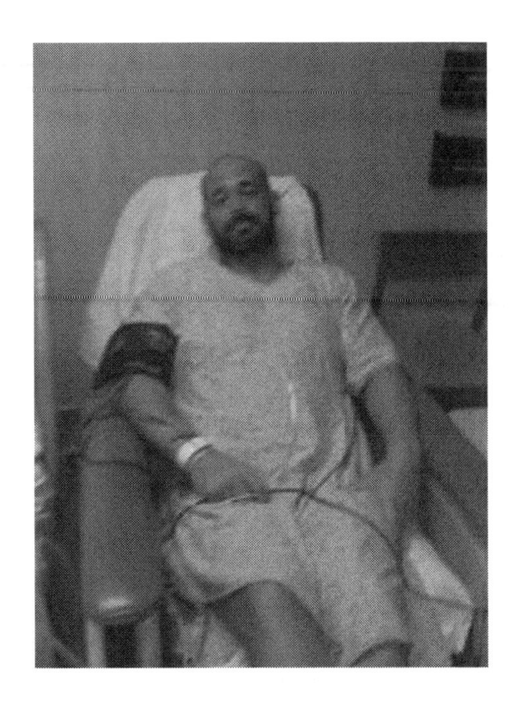

Dear Family and Friends,

I'm going to start with the pretty good news first. Finally the thorough lab analysis came back for Bob's bone marrow. Here's the scoop—Bob has acute myeloid leukemia in subgroup M4 with an inversion of the M16 chromosome. Per the lab results, it says, "This is associated with a better prognosis than most other AML subtypes." So that's my good news.

The bad news is that Bob still isn't eating. I guilted him into drinking an Ensure, but that's about it. The only good thing is that he's drinking a ton of water. He has a fever again, which he's had on and off for the majority of the day, and they are doing the ice thing again. In addition, they've given him more blood, more platelets, and now more blood again. They're also adding in potassium, Dilaudid, MS Contin, Zofran, Tylenol, and Protonix for good measure. I'm spending another night sleeping in Bob's room with him. They have a pull-out bed, and I'm sleeping with a surgical mask on. It's definitely something you have to get used to.

It's a blessing I have tomorrow off so that I can spend time with Bob. Thanks again to everyone for the prayers and kind thoughts.

— Michele

The good news was my cancer wasn't as bad as some others. It also has a lower requirement for transplants, which made me feel a little better. But I hadn't eaten in days, and I was in horrible pain. So even good news didn't affect me much. The fever proved to be a large part of my daily life for the near future. I was again buried in ice bags. Keep in mind, hospitals don't use "zip lock" type bags for ice. They have their own bags that have a string tie system. Well, the string never stays shut, and you get ice water leaking everywhere. I was miserable to start with, but that day seemed to be worse than usual. I couldn't move, I was in pain, and now I had ice water all over my bed.

This is the point where things start getting fuzzy for me. With all the drugs, I was in and out. Not really asleep but kind of in a haze. I wasn't complaining because it made the pain easier, but I became less and less involved in my care and decisions. Michele began taking on much of this burden.

Looking back on it now, Michele had it harder than I did. You see, I just had to take the pain. That was my part. Just suck it up and take the pain. Michele had to deal with the emotions of watching me go through all this as well as make all the medical decisions. Soon she would also have to deal with all of my personal finances and insurance. I don't know how she did it all. Through it all, she stayed so strong. I'm not sure I could have done it. Could you?

I tried to block out all of the stuff going on around me. I continued to see my life flash before me. What should I have done differently to prevent this? I tried so hard to become involved in the television. I needed something to get my mind off of this whole thing, but all I had was a hospital bed, fear, and pain.

SATURDAY, JULY 4, 2009

Happy 4th of July

Dear Family and Friends,

Bob is slowly getting his appetite back. He is drinking PowerAde and Ensure and eating cookies. At least it's a start. He's still in a lot of pain, but the diarrhea and fevers are beginning to subside. However, he still requires infusions of blood and plasma daily. If I had to guess, I'd say Bob weighs about 215 lbs.

Thanks to my family who had me over to briefly celebrate the 4th. And a super special thanks to Bob's friend Ron who is getting gift certificates for rounds of golf in south Florida, which he'll auction off in order to raise money for Bob's medical expenses. If anyone out there is a golfer, let me know, and I'll put you in touch with Ron.

Happy 4th of July everyone!

— Michele

I was feeling a little bit better but not much. I was trying hard to fake it while Michele was there. It was nice to have a day without the ice bags. I've learned to despise ice bags, but I wasn't in any way done with them. I had now lost about 35 lbs in half a month or so. Ron was my boss and he proved to be a true friend throughout this ordeal.

On the 4th of July down here in Florida, they show the fireworks on television, partly because it's hard to find parking to get close enough to see them and partly because it's 100 degrees in July. I decided I needed to watch the fireworks on television. I also decided that I was going to time my pain medicines so they were administered right before the fireworks were scheduled to start. Well, it was a great show, and I wasn't in too much pain. For twenty minutes, I was normal again. I remember smiling. I hadn't smiled in a while. What had my life come to? How did it get here?

I remember watching the fireworks and thinking, "Is this my last 4th of July? Is this how life ends?" I felt so alone sitting in that room. I couldn't get up, and I couldn't escape. I could only think and suffer. I knew this wasn't how I wanted my life to end, but could I really do anything about it? I so desperately wanted to have control over my life again.

SUNDAY, JULY 5, 2009

Eleven days since the start of chemo

Dear Family and Friends,

The good news today is that Bob didn't need any platelets or blood transfusions. In addition, he has been drinking Gatorade most of the day and even had a milkshake. However, I'm concerned that he's a little jaundiced because his eyes are yellow. I addressed it with the doctor this morning, and they're going to give him a liver ultrasound sometime tonight because his bilirubin levels are above normal.

Also, we finally got the webcam up and working so Bob could see his son, Christopher. Bob wanted me to tell everyone that he was tired and weak, but he was pushing forward.

Thanks for the prayers and well wishes.

P.S. Because I know everyone wants to come and see Bob, we could kill two birds with one stone and have a big welcome home/engagement party once Bob gets out of here. I'll let everyone know more later.

— Michele

A day without seeing a big, red bag hanging above me. At this point, I was used to seeing the IV and all the different colored drugs, blood, and platelets. Michele never told me about the jaundice and it was probably better. I had enough to worry about. The webcam is a great invention. It allowed me to stay in touch with CT without him having to come see how really bad I must have looked.

I didn't want my son seeing me with tubes and blood hanging all over me. I didn't want him to be scared. I'm sure a six year old has no idea what leukemia or cancer is, but he surely would know what blood looked like and that it was plugged into his dad's arm.

If I died, would his memories be of me dying in a hospital bed? Would he remember all the great fun we had? Would he know how much his father loved him, or would he just forget about me? Would he feel like his father left him? Would he think I wasn't strong enough? How would he remember me? I wanted to say so much to him in case I died, but I knew he wouldn't understand at his age.

Michele had been reading me all of the emails and comments from the blog. Many people wanted to come see me, but I didn't want anyone to see me like this. At this point, the amount of people I was in actual contact with was small. They were my family and lifelong friends. My dad once told me that I would judge my close friends by those who I could trust my son with. That's a small group of people. Yes, I'm an extremely overprotective father, but that's the group who would carry me through. In a way, I closed ranks so to speak. I only had so much energy, so my support group was small. Dave Tate was the biggest part of that group. Dave and I worked out together at Westside Barbell, probably the most famous powerlifting gym in the country at the time. Dave and I became close friends and have helped each other through many of life's issues.

Here's an email I sent to Dave. I think it demonstrates how close we are.

> *Dave,*
>
> *I do need a favor. It's actually the "big one." If anything goes wrong, I need you to check in on Chris for me.*
>
> *Thank you,*
>
> *— Bob*

Here was his response:

> *I will watch over him like he is my own, but you and I know I won't need to. I do understand why you're asking, and I would do the same.*
>
> *I'm glad to hear you touched bases with Alwyn. He (as well as you) is one of the strongest and most honest people I know. You have a very strong support system that is here for you for whatever you need.*

Just as Alwyn had jumped in this hole with me, Dave dove in as well, head first. There were times Dave literally had to carry me. I'm forever indebted to him. I couldn't ask for a better person to help carry me. How do you repay that type of friendship?

I needed to know someone would be able to tell CT about his dad and the kind of person I had been. I needed to know that he would be taken care of. The thought of him having to grow up without me tore me apart. It just wasn't fair. But nothing going on around me was fair.

TUESDAY, JULY 7, 2009

Didn't get a chance to write last night...

Dear Family and Friends,

Had a sort of rough evening. Bob didn't need any blood or platelets again, but they did do a liver ultrasound. Although it came back OK, they are keeping a close eye on his liver and kidney functions because his blood count is so low. (And his eyes are still yellow.) I asked the doctor about trying to feed him with a tube, but she said there would be too many complications, so it's imperative that Bob eats as much as possible. The diarrhea has been an ongoing issue as well. He had more Ensures and a vanilla shake from Burger King, and he actually ate breakfast yesterday. So I think he's moving in the right direction.

He had an issue with his PICC line. They can no longer draw blood from it for testing. They have to draw blood by sticking him again, and he's getting bruises all over his arms. Lastly, I emailed the head of adult leukemia over at Dana Farber again to talk to him about both Bob and his mom having leukemia and how rare that is genetically. I'm waiting for a response. That's about it. Please keep the emails and comments coming. I read them to Bob daily. He gets the bone marrow test on Wednesday, so keep your fingers crossed. This test will tell us how successful the chemo was at eradicating the cancer cells.

— Michele

A PICC line is basically a central IV line that allows you to receive all your IV medicines without having to get a new shot. It has a port that allows for the drugs to be administered. It also is supposed to allow for blood draw. When they lost the ability to draw blood, it was like a kick in the stomach. It meant I had to get stuck a couple of times a day for blood draw. This gets old very quickly. I was still in a lot of pain, and what seemed like constant needle sticks just made it worse.

I started to feel like the odds were getting worse for me. Adversity kept smacking me in the face. I tried to meet each and every adverse situation on the surface, but it's so hard to continue to try and be strong when everything seems to be going in the wrong direction. It was only a couple of months ago that I had total control of my life. It now felt like I had none at all. How do you stay positive through all of this?

TUESDAY, JULY 7, 2009

Kidney and liver issues

Dear Family and Friends,

I spoke with Bob's oncologist today, and they're having concerns about Bob's kidney and liver functions. She brought in a nephrologist, who specializes in kidney issues, and he said that Bob's kidneys are malfunctioning due to the dehydration caused by the diarrhea. They decided to increase his IV fluid rate over the next 24 hours, but if his kidney function doesn't improve, there is a possibility he will need a course of dialysis.

As I said in the last blog, his bilirubin levels are elevated, which affect his liver. If this doesn't improve, they will do an MRI to determine the next course of action. He needed another platelet transfusion today as well.

I'm taking a half day of work tomorrow so that I can be here when the doctor performs the bone marrow aspiration in the afternoon. This will determine if the chemo worked. Bob is very weak today but did a great job drinking the Ensures. The doctor spoke to him about his food intake, and the dietitian came by. They have added an apple juice supplement called Enlive, which has 9 grams of protein. He'll be drinking four of these a day in addition to the four Ensures.

Please keep your fingers crossed for tomorrow. Thanks again for keeping Bob in your thoughts and prayers.

—Michele

This is where my downward spiral truly began. It would be a very long spiral. When your kidneys stop functioning properly, a whole host of things are likely to go wrong. I was in such a haze that all the bad stuff wasn't really registering with me. I should have known I was in deep shit. Well, even deeper shit. I was trying to drink as many of the Ensures and Enlives as possible, but every sip made me feel like I was going to vomit. Everyone kept telling me to drink, and my stomach kept telling me to puke. On top of that, the diarrhea was horrible.

I didn't have the strength to make it to the bathroom, so they had to put the pot under my butt in the bed. At the time, I thought this was the most dehumanizing thing I could go through. I was wrong, and it would get worse. Imagine having to lay in your own shit and you can't do anything about it. I couldn't wipe my butt. I couldn't do a damn thing but take it. How could I not be scared? All I could do was try to hide it. I don't know if I did or if everyone just played along. My life was on the line, and here I was laying in my own shit.

WEDNESDAY, JULY 8, 2009

Bone marrow aspiration

Dear Family and Friends,

First the good news—the nephrologist said that after doubling the amount of IV fluids, Bob's kidney and liver counts were better today. If this trend continues, he *won't* need dialysis. Bob also got his bone marrow testing today. I had to watch it and it was horrible. Imagine sticking a five-inch screwdriver into your back and scraping out a piece of bone or something like that.

They won't have the results of the bone marrow test for about a week. This will tell us if the chemotherapy worked.

Bob was pretty much out of it the whole day. He was very disoriented and didn't make a lot of sense. I watched him sleep just to make sure everything was OK because he hasn't been acting like this before. He has also come down with wicked hiccups, and it sounds like he's choking. The doctor prescribed him muscle relaxers for it. He also needed two more pints of blood and a unit of platelets.

Finally, they weighed Bob today. When Bob was diagnosed with leukemia fourteen days ago, he weighed 251 lbs. Now two weeks later, he's lost 43 lbs and is at 208 lbs. Thanks to everyone for keeping the comments and prayers coming for Bob.

— Michele

I'd like to tell you that Michele was exaggerating the bone marrow aspiration, but she wasn't. It was the most painful thing I had ever experienced. The Dr. was great and did her best to make this go as smoothly as possible, but it was nothing but pure pain. She took a huge needle and inserted it in the back of my hip. I couldn't see any of it, but I felt all of it. I could feel her scraping and struggling to get all the bone she needed. When she was done, I think I passed out from the pain.

When I woke up, I just wanted painkillers and more painkillers. I prayed for sleep. My hip was just killing me. Thank God they kept the pain medicines flowing. I was still in a great amount of pain. I even had the thought that I was in some kind of dream. This couldn't be real, could it? It had to be a nightmare. The problem was the nightmare wouldn't end. I knew it was real.

As for my weight, holy crap. I was shocked. I knew I would lose weight, but I had no idea it would be that much. It scared me, and everyone kept pleading with me to eat. Everyone except my stomach, which kept telling me to puke up whatever I put in it. The good thing about being bedridden was I couldn't see how I looked. I purposely didn't have a mirror anywhere near me. I think seeing what I looked like would have just scared me even more.

THURSDAY, JULY 9, 2009

Internal bleeding

Dear Family and Friends,

Bob isn't doing well tonight. He is pooping straight blood, so they're monitoring him very carefully for internal bleeding. He is incoherent, going in and out of consciousness, and he's very weak and shaky as well. Tonight by far has been the worst night. I've been very upset, and it was the first time I lost it in front of him. I was just scared because he's never bled that much.

They're going to hold off on the pain medicines for a few hours to see if that will help him come around. They are also giving him emergency platelets to help stop the bleeding. I'm going to sleep at the hospital tonight and take the day off tomorrow so that I can speak with his oncologist directly and possibly get his GI doctor in here as well. They are going to be taking stool samples and drawing blood throughout the night to test him. Please keep him in your prayers tonight.

— Michele

This is when I really can't remember much. Michele may have lost it, but I don't remember it. All I remember is telling her I was fine and everything would be OK. I didn't really mean it, and I knew I was in deep shit. I was crapping blood. All sorts of doctors kept coming in and out. Every time I sort of came to, they were running more blood into me. I knew none of this was good.

Whenever I was alone, I cried. I was so sad and angry. I prayed for someone to come into my room. I wished anyone would come so that I had to stop crying. I couldn't get away from it. The thought of dying was constant. How do you face dying when you know it is coming? What was I supposed to do? I searched for answers and I had none.

FRIDAY, JULY 10, 2009

4:00 a.m. and possible transfer to ICU

Dear Family and Friends,

It's 4:00 a.m. right now, and Bob hasn't stopped bleeding. His blood counts are very low and so is his blood pressure. They are just running the final labs on his blood now, but it looks like they may be transferring him back to the intensive care unit due to the extensive amount of blood loss. I will keep everyone posted as we learn more.

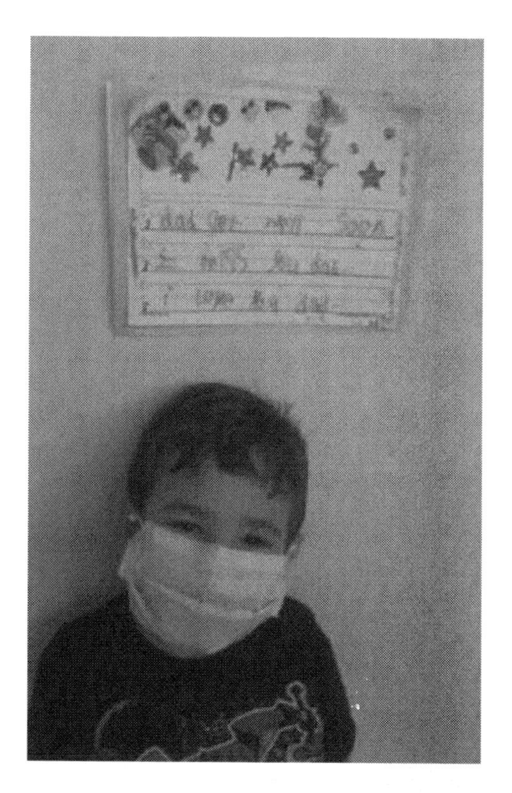

I forgot to tell everyone that Christopher came by last night to see his dad. I was so glad he came because you could see the happiness on Bob's face. I took a picture of Christopher standing in front of the 'Get Well' card he made for Bob.

Please say a prayer for Bob today.

— Michele

If I remember correctly, this is where my coma really started. I'd love to tell you that I remember seeing CT and that he gave me strength, but I don't. I'm sure in my subconscious he did, but from now through the next couple weeks, I was in a coma. I can't imagine how my family must have felt. There I was dying, and there wasn't a thing they could do.

As a side note, I have to be very honest here. It took me nine months until I could read this portion of Michele's blog. I started to and I just couldn't handle it. I had the easy part. I was out of it, and I didn't have to deal with the emotions of the situation. I finally sat down one night in April 2010 and read the whole blog, including all of the comments. I cried for four hours straight.

When friends and strangers encouraged me to write this book, they all emphasized a couple things. First, share how I was feeling. Second, share what I learned. Third, share my experience and how I got through it with others who may have to go through chemo.

The first thing I learned is that the love of one's family and friends can carry you through anything. My sickness brought all of these people in my life together. Through their strength and in the face of my adversity, I lived. I learned that when I couldn't walk my friends would carry me. When I couldn't breathe, my family would do it for me. No one ever gave up on me, and through their strength, I am here today.

Note: I won't add my comments to some of the following blog posts because I was in a coma and don't have anything to add.

FRIDAY, JULY 10, 2009

Bob in ICU

Dear Family and Friends,

Bob was moved to the ICU, and he isn't doing very well. They believe his bleeding is caused from the chemotherapy, which wears away the lining of the intestines and colon. We are waiting for the GI doctor to confirm where the bleeding is coming from. Please pray for him.

— Michele

FRIDAY, JULY 10, 2009

Fight of Bob's life

Dear Family and Friends,

It is 3:00 p.m. They've given Bob two pints of plasma and one bag of red blood, and he has three bags of red blood to go. The doctor thinks it's the chemo that eradiated his intestinal lining and colon or reopened the ulcers in his stomach. They said all they can do now is hope and pray that the blood takes and he doesn't bleed out. Today Bob is fighting for his life.

Please pray for him with all you have.

— Post from my iPhone

FRIDAY, JULY 10, 2009

Blood levels

Dear Family and Friends,

To give everyone an idea, normal platelet levels are at 150,000. Bob's are at 10,000. Your red blood cells/hemoglobin are supposed to be between 13–15 or something like that. Bob's are at four. He's fighting like hell though. Keep praying.

— Michele

SATURDAY, JULY 11, 2009

A lot of blood, a little bit of progress

Dear Family and Friends,

Yesterday they gave Bob blood, platelets, and plasma to try to increase his counts. They did go up a little bit but not as much as they had hoped. His blood is at 5.4, and his platelets are at 12,000. I spoke with the nurse this morning at around 6:00 a.m., and he said they are going to be taking Bob for another CT scan of his chest and stomach. It's 8:30 a.m. right now, and the doctor is coming soon.

I'm going to speak with her regarding his nutrition, as they wouldn't give him anything to eat yesterday at all, and he couldn't drink water until about 2:00 p.m. (Yesterday, they said that if his counts were up where they wanted them to be, they would give Bob nutrients in the IV. But they held off because they didn't want to tear up his stomach or intestines any more than they already are.) I will also get on my little soapbox and speak to his doctor regarding the importance of continuing to give Bob more blood products until he can maintain them at normal levels. My fear is that possibly the doctor will give up on Bob and stop giving him blood. Since two weeks ago, Bob has received blood from **thirty people**.

I want to thank the thirty strangers who, out of the kindness of their hearts, volunteered to donate blood and helped save Bob's life. Bob will probably need the help of thirty more people if not more. When I was in high school and college, I always donated blood whenever I saw a blood mobile, but in the twelve years since I graduated college, I've always made excuses not to. *Not anymore.* Every time the blood mobile stops by my office or I see it at the movie theater, mall, or wherever, I'm going to donate and hopefully help save someone's life.

Keep the prayers and thoughts coming for Bob. He's still got a long road ahead.

— Michele

Think about that for a minute—thirty strangers saved my life. People who I've never met and probably never will saved my life through their kindness. Due to what I've been through, I can no longer give blood, but I do ask that all of you do. The blood you give will save someone's father, mother, daughter, or son. The number of people's blood I received must be well over 100 by now. Each and every one of you has the chance to change someone's life. Please give blood.

SATURDAY, JULY 11, 2009

Blood in perspective, thanks Alwyn and Kim

Dear Family and Friends,

I'll admit I was a little disappointed this morning when the progress wasn't as much as I'd hoped, but I got a call from Bob's powerlifting friend, Alwyn, who put things in perspective. He said, "You have to look at it like Bob has gained 20 percent since yesterday and that's fantastic." Then he told me that although the numbers seem low for an average person, they are within range for someone going through leukemia. Kim also said the same. Both Kim and Alwyn have both gone through this themselves so their perspective is invaluable. I definitely needed to hear it.

As far as the blood donations are concerned, I don't think you can specifically donate in Bob's name, but you're paying it forward. If you want, you can donate and send him a card to let him know you did it in his name.

Thanks again to everyone for everything.

P. S. I spoke to the Dr. She's great. She said she's fighting for him tooth and nail. She's willing to give him an unlimited supply of blood products as long as he can take it. (I also put up a big 'Thank You' sign in the room with an 8 X 10 photo of Bob and Chris to humanize Bob to the nurses so they'll go the extra mile. I think it's working.) Also, they fixed his PICC line so the blood is coming into him faster, which means he can get more. The doctors are very happy about that.

— Michele

I have no idea how Michele made it through all of this, and we are only beginning. Her strength in the face of adversity was well beyond my comprehension. I can't begin to imagine how she continued to maintain her strength and positive attitude in the face of how sick I was. I also know that if it weren't for the support of people like Alwyn and Kim, she may not have been able to make it through this.

The Dr. was incredible. What a phenomenal woman she is. I'm sure I kept her away from sleeping and spending time with her family. Never once did she waiver in her support of me. She fought for me, and she still does to this day. Another thing about the Dr. that I didn't know then—she was pregnant at this time. She is an incredible woman. If I get a vote, she should be doctor of the century.

SATURDAY, JULY 11, 2009

Updated blood counts

Dear Family and Friends,

He went down from this morning, but I'm still trying to be positive.

Here are the counts:

- WBC, 0.3
- RBC, 1.56
- HGB, 4.5
- HCT, 135
- PLT, 11,000

You can go to this website to get an idea of where they should be: www.bymyside.com/infection/understanding.jsp.

Right now, Bob and I are in nuclear medicine, and they are doing a GI bleed test. They're trying to find out where the bleed is coming from (not that they can do anything about it), but it makes me angry. When I brought Bob into the hospital fifteen days ago, why didn't they do this test then before the damn chemo? Why wouldn't they fix the bleed before chemo started? I know hindsight is 20/20, but I would think they would have addressed this if he were at Dana Farber or something.

Also, coincidentally, I ran to the store while Bob was sleeping, and there it was in front of the Winn Dixie—the blood mobile. Now if I didn't at least try to donate, I would be a hypocrite. They said I didn't qualify for twelve months because Bob and I went to Honduras, but they did say I could hold a blood drive in Bob's honor and any blood collected will go to him. So I'm going to place a call on Monday and arrange for a drive at both my office and at Bob's office.

I hope Bob's counts go up and they find the source of the bleeding. Keep up the prayers for Bob. He isn't out of the woods yet.

— Michele

SUNDAY, JULY 12, 2009

Platelets better, breathing not great

Dear Family and Friends,

I spoke with the Dr. last night about Bob's bleed test. She said it isn't a specific test and that the endoscopy is much better. They can't do another endoscopy because the scope would tear his throat. So they are pretty sure the bleeding is coming from his stomach and bowel, most likely from the ulcers. They added a Protonix drip for the stomach acid and some type of coating for his stomach lining. I called at 6:00 a.m. and they told me his platelets had gone up to 47,000, which is a big improvement. However, the red blood cells are still low.

Then Bob's breathing became very garbled. I got the nurse, and they did a chest x-ray. They think he may have fluid in his lungs due to the amount of IV products they have been giving him. They stopped all IV except the blood and antibiotics. We are waiting for the results of the chest x-ray to see what the next step will be. They hope he will just need diuretics to drain some fluid, but they aren't sure. He has edema as well. They just put him on oxygen because he said he's having difficulty breathing, and they made him sit upright. But the good news is his O2 is steady at 99.

I'd like to give a special thank you to Ed Rectenwald and all the guys at his gym in Ft. Meyers. Ed told me today that they will be holding their upcoming meet for Bob and donating proceeds to his medical expenses. Thank you again.

Please keep Bob in your prayers. Thank you to everyone for all the kind words of hope and encouragement.

— Michele

Are you seeing a theme here? Murphy's law ruled my life for many weeks. Anything that could go wrong would go wrong. Ed Rectenwald is one of my closest friends. When I moved back to Florida in 2000, I started a small powerlifting gym. The original members—Ed, Doug Hollis, and Lance Mosley—were members of the handful of people I communicated with over the next five months. It was the daily emails from these guys just bullshitting that kept me going.

SUNDAY, JULY 12, 2009

Turn for worse

Dear Family and Friends,

This afternoon I noticed that Bob's breathing was garbled. They did a chest x-ray, but everything looked OK. I insisted on a pulmonologist. She said Bob has pneumonia and that he was retaining fluid in his esophagus. His blood counts also dropped way back down, and because he hadn't eaten in four days, they would have to put a feeding tube up his nose. They said they couldn't drain the fluid because they could tear something. When they put the feeding tube down, they couldn't get it all the way, and Bob started vomiting stomach acid. Some of it got into his lungs. His heart rate skyrocketed, his oxygen dropped, and his breathing became labored. He was really scared, and so was I. They put a mask on him, but it didn't help. The pulmonologist decided they needed to put him on a breathing machine.

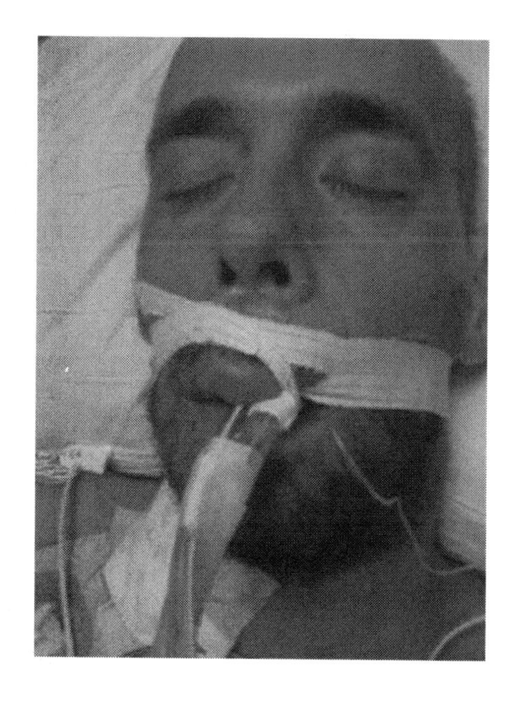

Bob is unconscious now. He has pneumonia, and his temperature is 103° F. They packed him with ice to try to lower the fever. They said it's hour by hour now. A priest came in to pray with him and then they made us leave. I told Bob not to be afraid and that everyone loves him.

Please say a prayer for Bobby.

— Michele

I wish I could tell you what it's like to have the last rites read to you, but I don't have a clue. I wish I could tell you I felt some higher power and dug deeper to live, but the truth is I was out of it still. I don't know if the Big Guy upstairs wasn't ready for me yet or if it just wasn't my time. I'd like to think the decision I made on that second day to live carried me through, but in the end, I think it was the power of my friends and family. Like I said, I wasn't ready to die. My son, fiancée, family, and friends still needed me. What else could I do but fight?

MONDAY, JULY 13, 2009

Monday morning

Dear Family and Friends,

They got Bob's fever down to 101° F at about 2:00 a.m., and they had to immediately give him platelets because his numbers dropped to 5000. They were able to bring that number to 22,000, but now Bob has a fungal infection in his blood. They have to change his PICC line because that's where they think it's coming from. They will also try to feed him through that line as well. Finally, they removed one liter of fluid from his stomach.

I spoke to Alwyn last night and he said this: "Now isn't the time for sadness or mourning. Now is the time to get angry and fight. And fight hard."

Let's all fight for Bob today. I know he's fighting too.

— Michele

Well, the last rites would have to wait. Apparently, I really wasn't ready to go yet, although that damn Murphy kept throwing everything he had at me. I'm sure Alwyn told Michele to tell me to fight. I'm also sure there were many more four-letter words in his statement with that beautiful Scottish accent of his.

It was people like Alwyn and my dad reminding me to fight that got me to fight so hard. When I felt like giving up, they wouldn't let me. My mom told me to just suck it up and that my son needed me. So many people told me to fight. I often questioned if I had the fight in me. My friends and family made sure I knew that there wasn't any other alternative. If I wanted to live, I had to earn the right and fight.

MONDAY, JULY 13, 2009

Not so good news and great news

Dear Family and Friends,

Bob is still on the respirator. The not so good news is that his liver and kidneys aren't doing great. They took him off the sedation this morning at 9:00 a.m., and as of yet, he still hasn't woken up. They are concerned but think it may be due to his liver function. They put him on wrist restraints in the event that he wakes up and tries to pull out the tube. Due to the fact that it's taken so long for him to come to, they don't want to sedate him again. As a precautionary measure, they are going to do a CT scan of his brain in about an hour to make sure he isn't bleeding. There is hope. Bob has groggily opened his eyes and grimaced when they gave him a shot. He also squeezed a hand. However, they're looking for him to squeeze a hand on command, which he hasn't been able to do.

Also, they have been giving him red blood all day. Now he will get two units of platelets, and they will do a blood test. They say the results of this test will be a sign of what his chances are. I'm praying they come back good.

Now for the great news—the bone marrow test came back without any leukemia! The Dr. said that if Bob can pull through this, he will make it!

Keep pulling for him.

P.S. I have the video recorder playing home movies of our Christmas so he can hear Christopher's voice. It seems to calm him. I'll write later tonight to tell everyone the results of the blood test.

— Michele

I'm running out of stuff that can fail at this point. Can't I get a freaking break here? My liver and kidneys are failing, and I'm still bleeding like a stuck pig. It doesn't surprise me that the shots were about the only thing that caused me to react. I hate shots. You can only take so many shots. I have no idea how the leukemia stayed in remission through all this. Maybe my luck was starting to turn? Is this the break I needed?

TUESDAY, JULY 14, 2009

No bleed in brain but infection in blood

Dear Family and Friends,

For the good news, Bob's blood counts have shot up to 8.4 and 31,000 for the hemoglobin and platelets, which is good. They also did a CT scan last night to see if Bob was bleeding in his brain, and the preliminary tests came back negative. Yesterday morning they took Bob off the sedation, and they were waiting for him to wake up and respond. Bob's Uncle Tommy came to visit him last night, and after twelve hours, Bob opened his eyes and started shaking his head to try to get the tube out. Although he couldn't respond to commands like "squeeze my hand," he did respond to Uncle Tom's voice. They had to sedate him again last night so they could perform the CT.

Because it wasn't a bleed in the brain that was causing Bob to remain unconscious for such a long period of time, they believe it was due to the fact that his kidney and liver function have gone south. I'm going to speak with the kidney doctor this morning to see if they will put him on dialysis. In addition, right after they sedated him last night, he spiked a fever of 102° F. However, they were able to control it by this morning.

The bad news is Bob has a systemic fungemia in his blood. This blood infection is very serious. The infectious disease doctor took samples of Bob's blood this morning to grow in a Petri dish to determine which antibiotics will kill the infection. "Also known as an 'opportunistic' infection or systemic candidiasis, it is a grave overgrowth condition where Candida penetrates into the deeper areas of the body. It occurs when Candida evolves from its normal state of yeast to a type of fungus that invades the blood circulation, liver, and urinary tract. Upon a systemic yeast infection happening, Candida starts to invade all body parts and organs, including the digestive system, respiratory system, eyes, liver, esophagus, skin, and blood. There isn't any single cause for a systemic yeast infection, and it can be provoked by different internal situations including a compromised immune system, deficient white blood corpuscles (granulocytopenia), and benign bacteria loss" (taken from buzzle.com).

Bob is far from being out of the woods, but I believe he is getting there slowly. Everyone knows he's a fighter. I'd like to thank everyone who has been donating to Bob's medical expenses. I just started to send out 'Thank You' cards. All the help is so appreciated.

Please keep the prayers coming for Bob.

— Michele

My Uncle Tom has been a huge part of my life. My son got his middle name from him. My Uncle Tom and Aunt April were like second parents to me. Growing up, I think I spent as much time at their house as I did at my parents. Uncle Tom has one of those booming voices and an even louder laugh. I was told he was the only voice who could get me to react when I was in a coma. They have a second home near our house, and I thank God for them. They made Michele dinner almost every night because they live so close to the hospital. Michele also got her little bit of sleep on their couch.

TUESDAY, JULY 14, 2009

Bob on dialysis

Dear Family and Friends,

When I arrived at the hospital this morning, they told me Bob's kidneys aren't processing as much as they would like. Because they had started to feed Bob through the IV, they're also growing the blood infection. Their only choice was to start dialysis. They hope this will get his kidneys functioning better and relieve the edema in his hands and feet. I've never seen Bob this bloated, even when he was powerlifting.

The kidney doctor didn't feel comfortable putting the dialysis line in Bob because he had to either stick it in the carotid artery in his neck or in the artery in his groin. Bob's blood is so thin that any little nick could be huge. They decided to use a surgeon to do it and chose to temporarily stick the line in his groin because this is less likely to damage something. They can only put the dialysis line in for 48 hours because the likelihood of infection increases in that area. In 48 hours, they will reassess the situation. If Bob's counts go up, they will bring him into surgery and put a permanent line near his neck.

Bob is still on a breathing machine and isn't conscious. However, he is responsive to outside stimuli like pain or the sound of people's voices. It's a catch 22 though because if you do talk loudly and he recognizes your voice, he wakes up groggily but is scared because he has the tubes in his throat. He’s confused and you can see him wincing in pain and trying to shake his head to get the tubes out. Also, Bob still has a high-grade fever.

Special thanks to Jim Wendler, Bob's powerlifting buddy, and Billy Lynch, Bob's roommate in high school. They’ve both been like brothers to him and have comforted me and Bob's family during the past few days.

Also thanks for the rest of the donations that came in today for Bob's care. Everyone's kindness has been overwhelming.

Thanks again and keep the prayers coming.

P.S. Today's picture is for the people from Bob's high school. Believe it or not, Bob's the one holding the silver championship cup.

— Michele

I was still full out in a coma, but just reading about a line in my groin makes me cringe. I now had lines in my nose, mouth, both arms, and my groin. I must have looked like one of the Borg from Star Trek.

Two of my very good friends came down to help my family. Bill Lynch was my roommate in high school. He can talk your ear off. I think we got along so well because I never talk and he doesn't stop talking. He has always been close to my family and is someone I've always been able to count on. Jim Wendler is one of those guys you need to meet. He's a cross between Mark Twain and a Hell's Angel. He's extremely bright and is covered with tattoos. I've always said that Dave Tate is the big brother I never had and Jim is the little brother I never had. It still amazes me how my family came together to get through this with me.

WEDNESDAY, JULY 15, 2009

Four liters

Dear Family and Friends,

Yesterday's dialysis was a success. They were able to drain four liters of fluid from Bob's body. His kidney function is still down, so they will have to repeat the dialysis again today. As far as his blood counts are concerned, I'm happy to report that his red blood cells are at 9.8 and his platelets are at 40,000. His white blood cells also jumped from 0.2 to 0.7.

Bob is still sedated and fought another fever last night. I got a little angry with the nurses because the air conditioning in Bob's room is broken and it was 78° F in there. Our normal air conditioning is set at 68° F. No wonder he is so damn hot. I had the nurses put in a work order, so we'll see if they can fix it today.

Thanks again to everyone for everything. All the kind words, prayers, and stories about how Bob touched people's lives mean so much.

P.S. Sorry I don't have a photo on my computer of Bob and the guys up in Ohio. I will look for one (in all my spare time) and try to post one soon.

— Michele

THURSDAY, JULY 16, 2009

No surgery today

Dear Family and Friends,

Sorry it's taken me so long to update this today, but I'm having a rough time for some reason. I think spending all this time at the hospital coupled with the fact that I can't sleep probably has something to do with it. It's just catching up with me.

Anyway, enough about me. Bob is hanging tough. They took 2.75 liters off him with dialysis this morning, but the surgeon thought with his low platelets, it would be too risky to do the surgery today. They will reassess in the morning. Bob's red blood cells are still decent, and the really good news is it looks like he's kicked the blood infection. Now we just have to get his kidneys up and running, stop all the fevers, raise the platelets and plasma, and get him breathing on his own without life support. The Dr. says that she sees little improvements every day and he's headed in the right direction.

Thanks to all of Bob's friends and mine for the encouraging emails and comments. It's amazing how you can see people's true colors in the face of adversity.

Keep praying for him.

— Michele

Hmm, Michele was having a tough time? I still say she had it harder than I did. I was in a coma and couldn't really feel anything. I don't remember this time at all. I'll never know how she was able to deal with the emotions. All I had to do was take the physical pain. The emotional roller coaster she had to ride must have been unbearable.

FRIDAY, JULY 17, 2009

Bob in surgery

Dear Family and Friends,

The surgeon stopped by early this morning and said that Bob was cleared for surgery because he has been maintaining his blood counts. His red blood is up to 9.1, his platelets are at 50,000, and his white blood is at 1.4. The main hurdle we're dealing with today is his kidneys. His creatine is very high, and for the first time yesterday, his urine was brown.

They said the surgery should last forty minutes. I'm sitting patiently in the OR waiting room with his Aunt April. Additionally, I spoke to the pulmonologist this morning to ask how long they think Bob will be on the respirator. She said that's the last thing they'll worry about. He could be unconscious for possibly another two weeks. They will analyze him daily.

Bob still has a low-grade fever, but the swelling from the edema is going down. Please continue to keep him in your prayers.

Love and thanks,

— Michele

FRIDAY, JULY 17, 2009

Surgery a success

Dear Family and Friends,

They successfully installed the port in Bob's neck, and they are doing another round of dialysis. The nephrologist said that right now his kidneys have shut down, but because he's young, they hope he'll recover in a few weeks, so the dialysis won't be permanent.

Bob's Aunt April was sweet enough to kidnap me and take me to lunch and a movie because they kicked us out during dialysis.

Love and thanks,

— Michele

SATURDAY, JULY 18, 2009

Bob is bleeding again

Dear Family and Friends,

I think Bob's sister Cindi said it best today—I'm bummed. During the night, Bob started bleeding in his poop again and lost two pints of blood. His white blood cells dropped by 25 percent. He maintains a low-grade fever as well. In addition, they had to increase his sedation to include Diprivan and Versed. I'm just sitting here with him waiting for them to start the dialysis. They will be giving him more blood and plasma. I'll write more later.

Love and thanks,

— Michele

My sister Cindi was down for the week. I don't think my friends and family planned it, but there seemed to be a new member of the support team coming to Florida every week. I'm sure it made it easier on everyone. My sister proved to be Michele's sounding board when it came time to make further medical decisions. My sister had been through this with my mom, and she has a lot of knowledge and experience when it comes to leukemia treatment.

MONDAY, JULY 20, 2009

Endoscopy scheduled for this morning

Dear Family and Friends,

It's Monday morning, and I got a lot of concerned emails from people yesterday wondering why I didn't update the blog. Pretty much everything stayed the same yesterday, and during the day, my parents invited Bob's whole family over to their new house for a cookout. We had a great time with my future in-laws but were disappointed Christopher couldn't attend.

As far as Bob is concerned, they decided to add Diprivan to his cocktail of sedatives. I'm not super happy about them giving him the "Michael Jackson" drug, but they have assured us that it's safe. Unfortunately, Bob has continued to bleed and more frequently. Fortunately, they say his blood counts are up high enough that they can do an endoscopy this morning. The GI doctor said he isn't sure if they'll be able to fix anything if they find something and that Bob could possibly have small bowel ischemia. However, they're still hoping it's just ulcers. For all the people who are following his blood counts, they are as follows: 8.0 for red (down from 9, which is from the bleeding), 3.2 for white, and 88,000 for the platelets.

I reluctantly signed the waivers for the endoscopy just now. They will be doing the procedure at 10:00 a.m. Then I have to go back to work. Because Bob is in the ICU and I had to take last week off as vacation, I'm hoping my employer understands. They told me before I left that they did.

That's about it. I'm really nervous about the procedure this morning. Please say a prayer for Bob.

Love and thanks,

— Michele

MONDAY, JULY 20, 2009

Endoscopy results, bleed in small bowel or colon

Dear Family and Friends,

The good news is the endoscopy went off without a hitch. The bad news is they didn't find anything. The bleeding from any stomach ulcer isn't enough to cause the massive amounts of blood in Bob's stool, so they have determined that the bleeding is either coming from the small bowel or the colon. Neither one is very good.

The next step is to do a three-hour bleed test where they inject his blood and wait to see where it bleeds out (he had one of these last week). It isn't a very specific test. Basically, they'll say, "Yes, he's bleeding and it's in the upper left quadrant (or something like that)." According to the GI doctor, after that, they will most likely have to do a angiography to determine exactly where the bleed is coming from. They may be able to cauterize at that point.

Everything is up in the air right now and none of it looks super fantastic. The best case is they're able to cauterize with angiography. The worst case is they have to do full on surgery and remove the bowel. They don't know if he's strong enough for that, but I'm jumping the gun. Bob is at 75 percent of a regular person's white blood, 60 percent of a person's red blood, and 50 percent normal on platelets.

I'm trying to be positive, but it's scary. I'd like to thank Bob's sister, Cindi, who is the most positive person in this whole thing. I don't know where it comes from, but man does she have strength. She's leaving to go back to Boston today, and I'm going to miss her. I told her I hope I don't see her again until Bob gets out of the hospital and we have a big party.

Please pray for Bob today. It's going to be a long day.

Love and thanks,

— Michele

TUESDAY, JULY 21, 2009

Angiography procedure today

Dear Family and Friends,

Last night, we had a long night with a new nurse who was too busy to be bothered with Bob's Aunt April, Uncle Tom, and me. Without going into too much detail, we had to report the nurse's behavior to both the nursing supervisor and the ICU director. That nurse will no longer be taking care of Bob. As of 6:00 a.m., Bob's counts have gone up. His platelets are up to 118,000, his white blood is up to 3.9, and his red is up to 8.4 (not as high as it was but better than yesterday when it was at 7.9).

The bleed test from yesterday came back positive, and they did determine that Bob has an active bleed in his small bowel. They believe it is limited to this area. The next step in trying to fix this is either to perform surgery and remove the affected bowel, which they don't recommend because Bob still isn't 100

percent, or do a less invasive angiography where a coil is inserted into his thigh and fished up into his bowel. They'll then inject the sites with dye to determine exactly where the bleed is coming from. While they are doing this, they will either try to embolize the bleed site or inject it with medicine to make it stop bleeding. The procedure should take about thirty minutes. Afterward, they will call to advise me of the successfulness of the procedure. At that time, I will speak to the GI doctor as well.

That's about it. Please pray for Bob. He's on the road to recovery. Stopping the bleed should hopefully be the last big hurdle. Love and thanks,

— Michele

This is where I acquired my permanent day nurse in the ICU. We'll call her Nurse E. Nurse E took such good care of me that I can never repay her. Don't get me wrong—she kicked my ass when I needed it, but she cared. In my book, that makes the good nurses and doctors. I'm sure it's a very demanding job emotionally, but some medical professionals simply don't give a shit.

Nurse E cared. She cared for me like I was a member of her family. There were many times I was down and needed to be pushed. Well, she pushed me. There were times when I needed someone to hold my hand or feed me. She did that too. She

always seemed to know what I needed. When it comes to ICU nurses, she's the best in my book.

TUESDAY, JULY 21, 2009

Still no idea where bleed is...

Dear Family and Friends,

They did the angiography today, but they couldn't find any active bleeding in Bob's small intestine. This sucks because the GI doctor is absolutely convinced it's the small intestine. His only solution is to keep giving Bob blood in the hopes it will stop. I tried to ask lots of questions to see if there is a possibility of an obstruction somewhere or if he's bleeding in other places, but the doctor was pretty adamant that he wasn't. Bob was bleeding all day. His red counts went down from 8.4 to 7.9, so I can't understand why that angiography didn't pick up a bleed. At this point, Bob received **50 pints of blood.** Maybe I should ask for a second opinion and possibly find someone who would be willing to look other places via a CT scan or sonogram or something. I spoke with Bob's sister Cindi and she agreed because neither one of us has an MD in gastroenterology.

Now for the super good news. Bob's white blood count is up to 4.9, which is within normal limits! In addition, his platelets jumped up to 157,000, which is within normal limits as well! This is a big step for him. He won't be needing platelets or plasma anymore—just packed red blood. We can theoretically go into his room without wearing gloves, but we aren't going to chance it for a few more days. Aunt April, Uncle Tom, and I will be going back to see Bob tonight and get an update. We can't go now because they are doing four hours of dialysis.

That's about it. Bob's bleeding is still a mystery, and hopefully we'll find an answer soon!

Love and thanks,

— Michele

WEDNESDAY, JULY 22, 2009

The mystery continues

Dear Family and Friends,

I want to make sure everyone realizes that Bob is still in a medically-induced coma and is on a breathing machine. I've been getting lots of emails and phone messages for Bob to call people. As much as I'd love for him to do that, it just isn't possible. That being said, Bob's doctors are happy with the progress he's been making with regards to his blood counts. Today he is up to 184,000 platelets, 4.8 white, and 8.6 red. He's doing so well that they've decided to keep his hospital room door open and not make anyone wear masks in his room. (I'm still a little bit leery on this one.) His oncologist didn't want him to get any red blood today, and I'm happy to report that there hasn't been any bleeding in the last ten hours. I hope this trend continues!

Now for the not so good news—although it looks like Bob has conquered the systemic yeast infection in his bloodstream, his doctors told me they have found the yeast colonizing in his spit (sputum) and it could possibly be in his lungs. In addition, his fevers are still ongoing, and they think this may be a factor. Bob is not out of the woods, but he is fighting hard. We are still on a holding pattern with regards to the mystery bleed in his small intestine. After speaking with the oncologist and nurse for a lengthy period of time, it seems that in addition to the ulcers initially found in his stomach, he may have had some ulcers in his small intestine that couldn't be detected in the initial testing and were caused by the overuse of anti-inflammatory medicines such as Advil and Aleve. The doctor couldn't stress enough what kind of damage overuse of these over-the-counter medicines can do. They believe the chemotherapy aggravated this area and they're hoping the bleeds resolve on their own. They will most likely repeat the angiography later on this week or early next week.

Please continue to keep Bob in your thoughts and prayers.

Love and thanks,

— Michele

THURSDAY, JULY 23, 2009

Pulling for Bob fundraiser

Dear Family and Friends,

Bob's friends at his old gym, Southside Barbell, and the Ft. Myers World Gym team will be putting on a backyard meet between the two gyms in a couple of weeks. They are planning to donate the proceeds to Bob's medical care. Stacey Motter, Ed Rectenwald, and Charlie Fay thought it would be a great idea to do a deadlift fundraiser where people can donate by the pound. They're going to give out fundraiser sheets for everyone competing on the teams so that they can get people to donate something. Even a penny a pound can add up. Although Charlie will be helping run the meet, he will also deadlift to raise money and should be good for a minimum of 700 lbs even if he has a bad day.

As far as Bob is concerned, his numbers looked fantastic last night, but he slipped this morning. Late last night, his platelets jumped to 250,000, his white cells jumped to 6.9, and his red cells, which were most impressive, jumped to 9.2. This meant that because they didn't give him any blood yesterday, he produced this on his own. The bad news is that when I woke up this morning and called, they said they repeated the test and his red blood had dropped to 8.2, which means he bled during the night. The other counts remained the same. They also reduced the amount of oxygen he needs from the breathing machine to 30 percent, which means he is slowly on his way to hopefully not needing it. (Cindi and I are hoping within a week.) Finally, they did another sonogram of his lower GI and liver this morning to try and pinpoint where this mystery bleed is coming from. Unfortunately, the results aren't in yet.

Lastly, I'd like to thank my aunt, uncle, and cousin in Baton Rouge, Louisiana, who sent in the largest donation to date for Bob's medical care. Their generosity, as well as the generosity of everyone who has been donating, is helping tremendously.

Keep praying for Bob. Love and thanks,

— Michele

It was very cool that my friends pulled together and helped raise money for me. When I decided to walk away from the powerlifting gym we started in Florida, Southside Barbell, I turned it over to Charlie Fay and Stacey Motter. They have done a great job with the gym. More importantly, I think Charlie and I exchanged texts daily once I got out of my coma. We have very similar political views, and the texts gave us both a chance to vent. I think Charlie was just trying to keep me busy, but it was much appreciated.

Around this time, many people started to ask if I had medical insurance. Yes, I did then and I do now. What most people don't realize is most insurance plans only cover 90 percent of your hospital expenses. My bills ended up well into the millions. So not only is cancer physically crippling, but it's financially crippling as well. Thank you to everyone who helped by donating.

THURSDAY, JULY 23, 2009

Bob to require bronchoscopy

Dear Family and Friends,

The doctors have decided ***not*** to give Bob dialysis today to see what happens. They are hoping his kidneys are strong enough to start processing fluids. In addition, the sonogram that was performed showed thickening of the gallbladder. The gastroenterologist wasn't too concerned, as he believed this may be caused from the food Bob is receiving in his IV (TPN). The GI doctor also seems to be convinced that Bob has stopped bleeding. I'm a bit leery of his assessment because his last three blood draws have been 9.5, 8.2, and 8.1. If they start increasing, I'll be a believer.

Finally, I spoke with the pulmonologist. She said she's concerned about the yeast in Bob's sputum. She said his lung secretions are thick and discolored, and he isn't able to pass them when he coughs into the breathing tube. Tomorrow she will be performing a bronchoscopy where they fish a line through his breathing tube and into his trachea and bronchial tubes to clean him out. He has been fighting a fever all day and sweating profusely. He just finally broke the fever and is at 99.8° F.

Please keep him in your thoughts and prayers.

P.S. People have been asking about blood donations. Here's some information.

To learn more about blood donation opportunities, visit www.givelife.org or call 1-800-GIVE-LIFE (1-800-448-3543). Someone needs blood every minute of every day. That blood can only come from a volunteer donor, a person like you who makes the choice to donate. There isn't any substitute for your donation. When you make a blood donation, you join a very select group. Currently, only three out of every 100 people in America donate blood" (from the American Red Cross, www.redcross.org).

Love and thanks,

— Michele

FRIDAY, JULY 24, 2009

Bleeding throughout the night...doctor wrong

Dear Family and Friends,

Bob bled significantly throughout the night. Three episodes. He went from 8.1 all the way down to 7.2. Since then, he has bled as well so it's probably lower. All that progress Bob had made and we're back to square one. They have to give him two units of blood this morning, and it looks like after the bronchoscopy, they will have to give him another angiography to try and find the bleeding. If Bob's GI doctor can't find the bleed today with the angiography, I'm going to throw a fit and insist on another GI doctor consult.

Please keep the prayers up for Bob.

Love and thanks,

— Michele

FRIDAY, JULY 24, 2009

Possible surgery tomorrow...source of bleed confirmed

Dear Family and Friends,

Today was a busy day for Bob. We started off with an angiography, and they did find that he was actively bleeding. However, they weren't sure if it was in the colon or small intestine. The GI doctor then performed a colonoscopy and finally determined it wasn't coming from the colon. However, he could see blood pooling from the small intestine. After this, they completed the bronchoscopy and removed a large amount of mucus from Bob's lungs. Then Aunt April and I met with the surgeon, and he said that if Bob can get his red count up today, they would consider surgery in the morning. They will make a small incision above his belly button, pull out 30 feet of intestine, try to find the bleed with a scope, and either cut or try to cauterize the affected part. We talked his oncologist into getting a second GI opinion, and the new doctor will be performing the surgery over the weekend if Bob is well enough. Bob is currently receiving dialysis, and because it's so late, we aren't able to see him again tonight.

In addition, I have *finally* been in touch with a blood coordinator at Florida Blood Centers. If you want to donate blood anywhere from Ocala to Ft. Meyers, Orlando to Ft. Lauderdale, please visit: www.floridasbloodcenters.org/donateNow/viewLocations.stml.

Your blood will go directly to Bob, so tell them you want to do a directed donation to Robert Youngs.

Please keep Bob in your prayers.

Love and thanks,

— Michele

SUNDAY, JULY 26, 2009

Eureka! They found it!!

Dear Family and Friends,

Sorry I didn't write yesterday, but it was a long day. Bob's Aunt April, Uncle Tom, and I sat with most of his doctors yesterday and decided that Bob was stable enough to have exploratory surgery to find out where the bleed in the small intestine was coming from. They did an enteroscopy this time where they fed a tube down his throat, past his stomach, and into his small intestine. The scope doesn't go the whole thirty feet of the small intestine, so the surgeon had to make an incision above Bob's belly button, pull out his intestines, and manually feed them through the scope for the GI doctor.

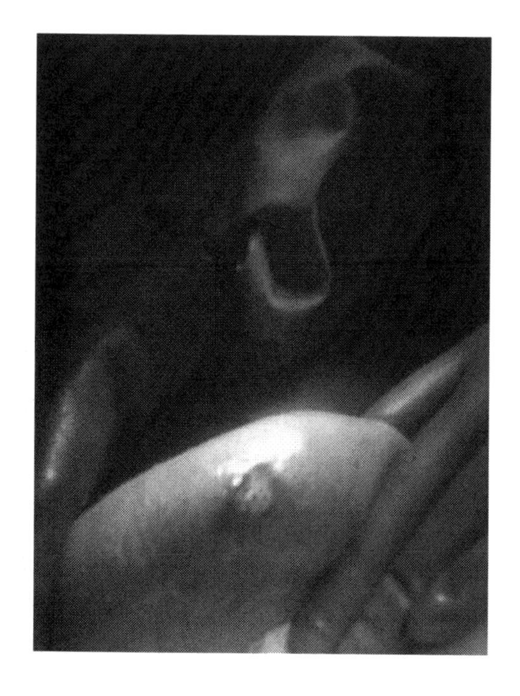

The doctor says the small intestine is like a sausage casing, and there aren't any problems feeding it through the tube. Anyway, they were worried that if Bob wasn't actively bleeding, they might not find anything. Boy, were they wrong! Normally, ulcers are found on the inside of the intestine. However, Bob's was so big that it ate through the inside and you could see it visibly on the outside. The doctors were relieved that they found it when they did because they said it could have torn open any day and Bob would have been in real trouble. The doctor said it was pretty rare to have the ulcer go all the way through, so he took a picture on his camera phone and sent it to me. They cut out 6–9 inches of his intestine in the affected area and reattached it with stitches and staples. They said the surgery went well. This was yesterday at 7:00 p.m.

Bob is back in his room recovering. He is still on a breathing machine and isn't conscious yet. As of this morning when I called the nurse, they said that during the night Bob had some more bloody stools, but they had expected it as residual from what was left in the intestine. The other thing is that during the night Bob's red cell count dropped from 9.3 to 7.9, but the nurse thinks that's from post-operation oozing of the repair site. They're giving him more blood right now as a precaution. I'm still worried but trying to be positive. I'm heading off to the hospital in a few minutes so I can meet with the surgeon.

Thanks to everyone for keeping Bob in your thoughts and prayers.

Love and thanks,

— Michele

It has nothing to do with where we are in the story, but I can tell you the removal of part of your intestine will give you gas. I now have gas like you wouldn't believe. I'm a farting machine. So be forewarned when you're around me. I also have a beautiful scar right down the middle of my belly. Every day when I look in the mirror, I'm reminded of what I went through.

This is also when I got my first scar from this whole ordeal. I will carry those scars for the rest of my life just as I will this experience. At times, it still haunts me. I cry often over what could have happened and what I felt was taken from me. My life will never be the same. The emotional scars don't show up in the mirror, but they fade a lot slower than the ones on the outside of my body. Can you imagine the baggage I carry?

MONDAY, JULY 27, 2009

Monday morning—possible tracheotomy

Dear Family and Friends,

Yesterday Bob was recovering from his surgery. He was still bleeding a lot, but the doctors and nurses assured us it's normal after surgery. He was also fighting a fever. By last night, his fever had subsided, and during the night, he only had one episode of bleeding (which is better than the six yesterday). The only thing is I'm waiting to speak to Bob's pulmonologist about a possible tracheotomy. I'm not thrilled about them cutting into Bob's neck, but the respiratory therapist told us yesterday that Bob's throat is irritated from the big tubes. The tracheotomy tubes are much smaller and will let him close his mouth.

He's been under now for fifteen days, and they usually only like patients to be under for fourteen days before they either wake them up or do a tracheotomy. The nurse said Bob should recover more quickly with it. I'll speak to the doctor this morning, and chances are they'll do the procedure today. If Bob stops bleeding altogether and stops having fevers, they will consider waking him up. He opened his eyes yesterday for about thirty seconds, and it breaks my heart because he looks confused and scared. I'll only be able to exhale a sigh of relief when he's fully awake and able to breathe on his own.

Please keep Bob in your prayers...he's almost there!

P.S. I know people want to see Bob, but he's still in intensive care and he isn't conscious. Both the hospital and I ask that only immediate family come visit him at this time until he wakes up. I know Bob wouldn't want anyone to see him like this. Thank you for your understanding.

Love and thanks,

— Michele

TUESDAY, JULY 28, 2009

Bob is *still bleeding*

Dear Family and Friends,

I'm very discouraged today. Bob tested positive for a bowel infection called clostridium difficile (C. diff). According to the Mayo Clinic (MayoClinic.com), "C. diff is a bacterium that can cause symptoms ranging from diarrhea to life-threatening inflammation of the colon. Illness from C. diff most commonly affects older adults in hospitals or in long-term care facilities and it typically occurs after use of antibiotic medications. In recent years, C. diff infections have become more frequent, more severe, and more difficult to treat." Because of this, they had to take out the PICC line in Bob's arm and switch it to his other arm. Now they have to take his blood pressure from his leg because his arms can't handle it.

To add insult to injury, I spoke with the doctors yesterday regarding Bob's surgery. I found out the whole truth, which made me very upset. When the GI doctor and surgeon performed Bob's operation on Saturday, they went down halfway into Bob's intestine, found that huge ulcer, and stopped. Come to find out, there was still fifteen feet of intestine they didn't look at with a scope. All they did was inspect it on the outside. If Bob has ulcers in his stomach and a huge ulcer in his intestine, I just don't understand why they didn't finish the job. When I asked them, they said it was too deep, and they were worried they might perforate the intestine. However, I didn't ask them why they just didn't take the scope out of Bob's mouth, stick it right at the site where they were cutting, and start there. They said they were confident that the spot where they cut was the culprit of all of Bob's problems.

I really hope they're right, but I'm a realist and don't believe this is the case. It's been two and a half days now since Bob's surgery and he's bleeding more frequently and with more volume. This concerns me. His platelets have dropped by 100,000 to 220,000, and although they are giving him blood—four units a day with plasma the last two days—his red blood count hasn't risen. I asked the surgeon if he was concerned, and he said he still believed Bob was bleeding out from his operation.

With regard to Bob's tracheotomy, I was surprised when I spoke to the pulmonologist yesterday. I was expecting her to make me sign the waivers to immediately do the tracheotomy. However, she said Bob's blood gas was in the normal range and he was only breathing with 20 percent oxygen, so she wanted to give him the benefit of the doubt, wake him up, and see if he could breathe on his own. She woke him up, and the good news is he's still with us. He can recognize faces and blink to communicate. However, yesterday they didn't believe he was strong enough to breathe on his own. The pulmonologist doctor said the surgeon would perform the tracheotomy operation. When I spoke to the surgeon, he wanted to do the tracheotomy on Thursday. He said he wanted Bob's bleeding issues to be handled first. I knew he was concerned about the bleeding, but I guess he just didn't want to admit it. So for the next two days, they're going to wake him up for an hour or so and see if possibly his breathing is getting stronger. Maybe he won't need the tracheotomy after all.

If you couldn't tell, I'm very upset at this whole bleeding situation. But every day I have to remind myself to be grateful for the little things Bob has accomplished. I'm grateful Bob can recognize people. This shows us that after fifteen days, he's still there. I'm grateful his blood gas is in the normal range. I'm grateful his kidneys are getting back to normal and he hasn't needed dialysis in the last three days. I'm grateful Alwyn Cosgrove called me yesterday and gave me a kick in the butt to keep me motivated, and most importantly, I'm grateful that no one, including the doctors, has given up hope. I appreciate all the kind words and support everyone is sending. To be honest, if I didn't have Bob's aunt and uncle here helping me get through this, I think I would have had a nervous breakdown by now. All the emails and words of encouragement have been wonderful. Thank you so much.

Bob has hit a rough patch and is still fighting like hell. Please continue to pray for him.

Love and thanks,

— Michele

They may have woken me up, but I don't remember it. I'm actually glad I don't remember. All of that crap in me would have freaked me out. Aunt April and Uncle Tom really did help carry Michele through. I learned just how strong my family is. Are you starting to see what I mean about Alwyn jumping in the hole with me? He always seems to be there at just the right time.

I'm still amazed how a tragedy can bring people together. So many people looked after Michele and me. Those same people continue to support us. You really do find out who you can count on when you face adversity. You also feel a debt that you can never repay. When I was so scared I was going to die, people stood up and wouldn't let me die. They stood by me and made sure I stayed in the fight.

WEDNESDAY, JULY 29, 2009

Bob is still fighting!

Dear Family and Friends,

I had the opportunity to speak with the GI doctor who did Bob's small intestine surgery on Saturday. I cornered him in the ICU and asked him to explain why he didn't go all the way to the bottom of Bob's intestine. He gave me a song and dance and blamed the surgeon, but he finally admitted they didn't look internally with the scope at 40 percent of Bob's small intestine and there was a good possibility Bob could have more ulcers there.

Speaking of ulcers, I then spoke with the pulmonary doctor who told me that Bob has an ulcer on his trachea. She said when Bob wakes up he may have to have this lasered in the future because it could lead to a narrowing of the area.

I didn't sleep much last night and called the nurse at 2:00 a.m. to see how Bob was doing. She said he needed a tube placed into his colon to collect all the bleeding because it was so frequent. Even though he was given four pints of blood yesterday and three plasmas, his counts still went down.

After hearing this news at 2:00 a.m., I couldn't sleep the rest of the night. I was very angry at the GI doctor for what I felt was a half-done job. I looked online at the best GI hospitals in the country. Massachusetts General ranked number four. I figured I'd get a quote to see how much it would cost to have Bob transferred there via ambulatory jet with ICU capabilities. The two quotes I received were $16,000 and $18,000. Needless to say, I spoke with his sister, and we're just going to keep him at Bethesda.

I went to the hospital this morning before work and saw Bob. He was asleep. I talked to him and tried to get some of the doctors on the phone. I insisted with the nurse that they perform a bleeding scan on him today. (They have it scheduled for 2:00 p.m.) Then I spoke with the infectious disease doctor. He said Bob's C. diff infection should last two weeks.

After I got to work, I called to check on Bob and was able to catch the pulmonologist again. She told me the results of the CT scan from last night. It showed that Bob has "necrotizing pneumonia" and some of his lung tissue is dying.

I asked her if Bob's blood counts were good enough for him to get the tracheotomy tomorrow. She said they were going to give him more blood, plasma, and vitamin K and she thought he could proceed tomorrow.

Surprisingly, she said Bob's breathing was doing pretty good and that she was going to lower the oxygen to 28 percent.

It amazes me that despite all the things being thrown at Bob, he's still kicking ass. Bob is a true fighter and is holding his own. I have to believe he's going to make it through!

Please continue to keep Bob in your thoughts and prayers.

Love and thanks,

— Michele

Tube in my colon? Yeah, the coma sounds like a good thing. I really wouldn't want to be awake for that. Michele later told me it was like having a PVC pipe in my butt. She must have been scared to death. Somehow in the coma I managed to keep fighting. I have no idea how I did that.

THURSDAY, JULY 30, 2009

Tracheotomy a success

Dear Family and Friends,

Last night, I brought a Christmas photo of Bob into his room and posted it up on the wall. When I called the night nurse this morning at 6:00 a.m. to find out when Bob's surgery was scheduled, she said she had a surprise for me. When April and I got to the hospital, we were surprised to find she had shaved Bob's face and head for us! (He hadn't had a shave in 37 days, and with the chemo, his hair was patchy. Now he looks like a skinnier version of the old Bob!)

Bob had the tracheotomy surgery today at 7:30 a.m. Although the doctor said he had to cauterize the majority of the area because Bob was bleeding more than average, the surgery was a success overall. They relocated the breathing tube, which also sucks lung mucus, from his mouth into the trach in his throat, and they moved the stomach tube from his mouth to his nose. For the first time in seventeen days, Bob will finally be able to close his mouth! Also, they have decided that because the trach is much less scary for him, they'll wake him up fully. They took him off the sedation medicine a few hours ago and he has his eyes open now, but it may take a day or so until he fully comes around. Then the weaning process can begin.

My mom and Aunt April were there this morning when the surgery finished. We were all sitting around with Bob while he was recovering, and the strangest thing happened. The GI doctor came into the room and said he spoke with the surgeon and the other GI doctor and that if Bob continues to show signs of bleeding, they will give him a "camera pill." He will swallow it so they can find the source of the bleed non-surgically using video. (I suggested this last week, but they told me it could only be done as an outpatient procedure.) Here is the strange thing. The doctor told me they were going to get the hospital to pick up the tab on the procedure. I'm not going to say no, but I also know there isn't any such thing as free. Maybe it's because I said I wanted to move Bob to another hospital with better technology. That's what I'm hoping at least. Anyway, I'm hoping the camera pill won't be necessary and Bob stops bleeding on his own. We're going to have to wait and see. Keep your fingers crossed!

P.S. I'd like to thank all the people in my office. They were nice enough to sign a card asking for a speedy recovery and send prayers and caring words for Bob among other things. It was very kind of them!

Love and thanks,

— Michele

FRIDAY, JULY 31, 2009

Eyes open and red tape

Dear Family and Friends,

Since yesterday, they've had Bob off the Versed (which is the medication they used to put him under). He has his eyes open, and he's making some progress like shaking his head yes and no. He can move his hands about an inch but will require extensive physical therapy. Bob's bleeding is still going on, and his red count (hemoglobin) went from 9.3 to 7.9 during the night. I pushed the nurses and GI doctor this morning to order the capsule endoscopy for Monday, and it's been approved by the GI doctor's office and Bob's insurance. However, we're still waiting on approval from the hospital. His kidney function is slowly getting better by the day, and he's off the dialysis. Other than that, everything else is the same. I can't begin to thank everyone enough for all the kind words, emails, and support.

Love and thanks,

— Michele

SATURDAY, AUGUST 1, 2009

Bob awake but blood pressure too high

Dear Family and Friends,

When I went to visit Bob today, he was significantly more awake and trying to mouth words to me. He is able to lift his hands if ever so briefly and wiggle his toes. I know that might not seem like much, but it's a huge improvement. His mom was able to see him for the first time in a week because she's been battling a bout of bronchitis, and with her previous leukemia and the fact that Bob still has the C. diff infection, they thought it wouldn't be safe.

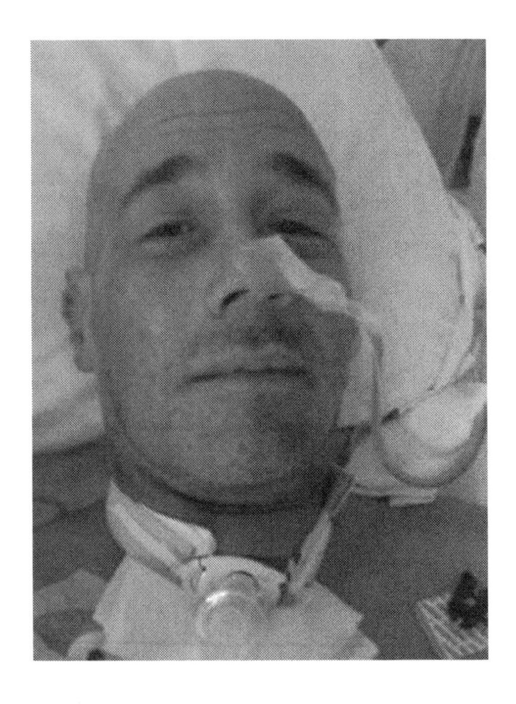

Here was the problem today. Bob was most likely still confused as to where he was and trying to deal with the pain of his stomach surgery, the bleeding, and the trach tube in his throat. He kept asking for water and PowerAde, but the nurses feared any fluids could restart the fungus previously growing in his lungs or the necrotizing pneumonia. They were also worried that he could aspirate, so they only allowed him a few ice chips. He was frustrated, and his blood pressure skyrocketed. They tried to give him a labetalol drip for the blood pressure, but it didn't work too well. Then they moved on to some patch that was supposed to help, but it was sporadic at best. Bob's blood pressure got to the point where it was 193/95, and Aunt April, Uncle Tom, and I decided it would be best to leave so he could get some rest. At that point, they had to call a cardiologist because nothing was working. In addition, the weekend oncologist decided to give him a blood clotting medicine in hopes of trying to stop the bleeding because the higher his blood pressure, the more he bled. The clotting medicine is called Amicar. It is used to treat excessive post-operative bleeding. Its side effects are mainly related to the gastrointestinal tract and include nausea, vomiting, abdominal pain, and diarrhea. Unfortunately, it didn't seem to help much.

I was fortunate because the day nurses let me help clean Bob after one of his bleeding episodes. Although it was hard to look at, I realized why they had to insert a tube into his colon. His backside looked like ground-up meat, a combination of what looked like rotting open wounds and bedsores. It's probably the grossest thing I've ever seen, and my heart broke for him. Although the nurses covered it with paste and tried to have him sit up today, I asked them if they could get a wound care person in there to treat it as soon as possible. The wound care person won't get there until Monday.

Dammit! I just got off the phone with the nurse like two seconds ago. Because of his high blood pressure, Bob's red blood hemoglobin plummeted to 6.8, and his white blood count is down to 5.9 (at least this is still in range). His platelets are low too at 91,000. The good news was the cardiologist put him on a Brevibloc drip just now, and his blood pressure is in the 140s. I'm hoping this slows the bleeding during the night. They are giving him two more units of blood and will retest at 4:00 a.m. I'll keep everyone updated. In the meanwhile, please say a prayer for Bob. He's awake and he's fighting. He's trying to get his strength back. He mouthed that he loved me today and that made all the difference in the world to me. I have hope he's going to pull through.

Love and thanks,

— Michele

I'm finally to a point that I can remember. Waking up from the coma was obviously great because I was alive, but I didn't really know I had almost died, so everyone seemed to be much more excited than I was. All I knew was that I was weak and had this damn tube in my throat. I've squatted 850 lbs, bench pressed 540 lbs, and deadlifted 705 lbs. I wasn't a weakling. However, I couldn't even lift my hands. I could barely move my fingers. I couldn't even speak. It was so damn frustrating. I couldn't speak, so I tried to write. Then I couldn't hold the pen to write. I got so upset at myself, my blood pressure skyrocketed.

I was so scared again. I was awake, but my body was betraying me. I really wondered if I could win this fight. So very much had gone wrong, but here I was. I don't know how I got through what I did. I just kept telling myself the hard part was done and I needed to keep fighting.

The water and ice became a big issue. It would still be a week or so until I could drink a little. My mouth felt like it had sand in it. I was so damn thirsty. I would have given anything to just swish something in my mouth. I've never been that thirsty in my life.

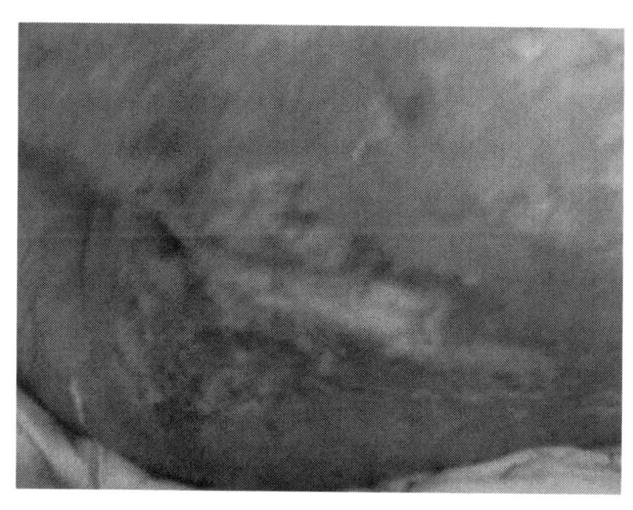

OK, let's talk about my butt. To this day, I still haven't looked at the pictures Michele took on her iPhone. I knew it was bad when the nurses rolled me over and said, "Holy shit." It hurt constantly and did for months. There was nothing I could do because I was so weak. I couldn't roll over or take pressure off the area. This is when my battle with chemo truly turned to a battle of taking pain. This first day was the hardest. I couldn't figure anything

out, and I couldn't move. I could see the remote to move the bed. It was inches from my hand. Why couldn't I just grab it? I tried to call out, but I had no voice. That night, I have never felt so alone or helpless in all my life. My night nurse came in to give me my medicines and was kind enough to help set the bed so my butt didn't throb so much. She put the remote for the bed and television in my hand—a little victory for me. The little victories kept adding up.

That night, I swore one thing to myself. I'd be damned if I was going to die covered in my own shit and blood. No sir. No way in hell. This wasn't any way for a human being to be treated while alive let alone have to die like that. It's funny how I had started to think of how I didn't want to die. Is there a good way to die? Probably not. I used anything I could to motivate myself to live.

MONDAY, AUGUST 3, 2009

Monday morning miracle????

Dear Family and Friends,

The last time I wrote was Saturday night. At that time, Bob's blood count had dropped into the high 6s range and his blood pressure was in the 190s, and they were going to start giving him new drugs for clotting and blood pressure. Apparently, all the stars aligned for Bob, and everything seemed to work. During the night on Saturday, they gave Bob two units of blood and two units of plasma and retook his blood counts Sunday morning. His blood counts jumped from 6.8 to 8.5. Although that was a big improvement, I was cautiously optimistic. They didn't give Bob any blood during the day yesterday, and his counts remained at 8.5. I was still cautiously optimistic about the clotting drug Amicar. They didn't give Bob any blood last night, and his blood counts went up on their own to 8.8. His platelets rose to 92,000, and his white blood cells rose to the 8s as well. In addition, Bob's blood pressure returned to the 130s as of last night, and when they did a chest x-ray, it came out normal for the very first time in the last three weeks. It looks like his pneumonia is gone. Everything is looking up for Bob today!

When we saw him yesterday, he was very alert. He wanted to know what the game plan was, and he did lots of exercises trying to move his hands and feet. Don't get me wrong—Bob still has severe edema in his hands and feet, and his range of motion is very minimal (he can't lift his hands and feet much, and he still can't hold a pencil), but he's trying and making a huge effort. If he continues on this path, he should be off the breathing machine within a week! Thanks to everyone for their prayers and well wishes for Bob. They seem to be working!

Love and thanks,

— Michele

I remember I had a conversation with the Dr. on this morning. You see, the Dr. came to see me every morning. I swear that woman worked eight days a week. We had a talk about where I was, a 'no bullshit, here is where you are' conversation. She laid it out, and it wasn't pretty. But I could do it, she said. She asked me what I needed. I simply said, "Keep my pain meds coming so I don't suffer too much, and I'll do my workouts." I told her I would do whatever I needed to do. She asked me what I needed from her, and I told her I needed her to never give up and to take care of the medical stuff.

Michele lists all of these numbers and what is normal and what isn't for blood counts. I still have no clue what any of the normal ranges are. I told the Dr. that she and Michele could take care of the numbers because I had no control over them.

I told her I would take care of what I had control over. First, I had to be able to move. Second, I had to be able to talk. Third, I had to take the pain. The rest of it was for her and Michele to deal with. Michele gave up telling me my numbers because she knew I couldn't care less. She spent hours worrying about the newest blood results and where they were. Me? It didn't matter. I had to get my hands to work first. So my dad brought in squeeze balls and things like that. I still remember the speech Jim Valvano, the famous North Carolina State basketball coach, gave on cancer and never giving up. He talked about all the stuff cancer could take away, but it could never take his mind. Well, cancer had taken its best shot at me, and I was still in the fight. In my mind, I was standing up on my bed giving cancer the finger with both hands.

This was a big day for me. I started to look at the things I needed to do to live. For the first time in a long time, I had stopped trying to avoid death and was instead trying to come up with a way to live. I didn't realize it then, but it was a big step.

TUESDAY, AUGUST 4, 2009

Tuesday afternoon and still no blood loss!

Dear Family and Friends,

It's Tuesday afternoon, and knock on wood, Bob still hasn't lost any blood. I spoke with the pulmonologist this morning as well as the infectious disease doctor and they both said Bob was heading in the right direction. A few minutes ago, I finally tracked down Bob's GI doctor, and we set up the capsule endoscopy for Wednesday morning. It should take twelve hours to get through him and then they'll have video. Even if it doesn't show active bleeding, it can at least show them possible trouble spots for the next round of consolidation chemotherapy that he'll need in a month or so (he's still in remission, but they do a short round of chemo as a precaution). As soon as the camera pill is done, they'll start weaning him from the ventilator and hopefully he'll be breathing on his own by Sunday. He'll still have the trach in for a month or so until he's fully healed. Finally, we're hoping Bob and his son Christopher can be reunited soon. Christopher has been anxious to see his dad, and I know seeing Chris would really lift Bob's spirits. Hopefully, we can get that done this weekend too.

I just wanted to say thank you to everyone who has been sending me emails. I promise I have read each and every one of them. Unfortunately, because I'm working full–time, going back and forth from the hospital three times a day, and keeping up with the blog, I just don't have the time to write everyone back. But I'm reading them all, and I appreciate all the kind words and prayers everyone is sending! Thank you again!

— Michele

I had such high hopes for the camera pill. I had received some of the details on the extent of my bleeding while I was out. I was really hoping this would tell the doctors where the bleed was so they could fix it. Then we could move forward with the chemo without the risk of more bleeding. Simply put, I was pissed. I felt like the doctors weren't pulling their end of the load.

I really wanted to see Christopher. I almost needed to see him. But I had tubes in both arms and a feeding tube in my nose, and I was on a ventilator. I think I would have scared him more than helped him. I couldn't speak or even move my hands. I didn't want his last picture of me to be this. It would have to wait.

THURSDAY, AUGUST 6, 2009

No results from camera pill yet

Dear Family and Friends,

I'm so sorry I didn't have a chance to write yesterday, but things were very hectic. The good news is Bob was the first person ever in the history of Bethesda hospital to get a capsule endoscopy. Everything went well, and I'm waiting for the results from the GI doctor sometime this morning to find out where the heck Bob is still slowly oozing blood. Bob has significantly decreased the amount of bloody stool he's producing, so they are going to take the tube out today. The bad news is he's still somehow bleeding. His blood went down to 7.9, and they're giving him two more pints of blood today. He is very alert and aware, which is a fantastic thing. However, now he has lots of questions and is getting very anxious.

He still is battling lung issues, which cause him to have a lot of mucus. When he's on the ventilator, it is very hard for him to cough it up. They took him off the ventilator yesterday for six hours and he did really well. It helped him cough up a lot of stuff, but it also made his stomach and back sore from all the coughing. While I was there this morning, he panicked on the ventilator because it felt like he was choking. The infectious disease doctor said he's getting better every day and took him off a few antibiotics. Bob also starts physical therapy today. I will blog again when I find out the results from the camera pill.

Thanks for keeping Bob in your thoughts and prayers.

Love and thanks,

— Michele

The pill was a blur. They kind of drugged me up and then got it down my throat. I really don't know how nor do I want to. I wanted to know where in the hell all of this blood was coming from. I had all these doctors coming and going and none of them could figure it out. It couldn't be that friggin' hard, could it?

Now for the mucus issue. When they took me off the ventilator, my job was basically to cough up as much phlegm and mucus as possible, but I couldn't do it like a normal person. I had to cough it up the trach hole, which has a tube running through it. So I coughed up huge amounts of crap all over the room. I mean I had a whole wall covered in crap. The poor cleaning people had to come in and clean my walls numerous times per day. I felt so bad that these nice people had to clean up that stuff. It was just nasty.

There were times when I felt like the mucus was going to choke me to death. I couldn't breathe, and I felt like I was never going to be able to breathe again. It scared me so much. My resolve continued to be tested on a daily basis. How could I stay positive?

THURSDAY, AUGUST 6, 2009

Camera pill a bust; no video taken

Dear Family and Friends,

The darn camera pill was a bust. I just got a call from the GI doctor's assistant, who said no video was taken. I said, "OK, just give him another one." But she said the doctor was on vacation. Just Bob's luck. Now I'm trying to get someone to get him another one of these camera pills, and I want to get a CT scan or an x-ray or something to make sure it isn't stuck inside of him. (He hasn't passed the pill yet.) So needless to say, it's been a pretty messed up day. They wanted to switch him from the IV fluids to feeding him from the tube in his nose, but they can't now until they get results letting them know that Bob isn't bleeding anymore.

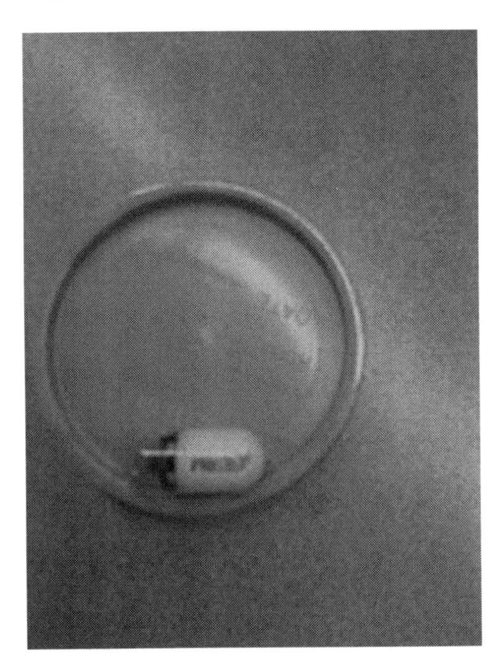

Please keep Bob in your thoughts, and I will update everyone when I know more. Love and thanks,

— Michele

I was pissed. I was just laying there in pain 24 hours a day and the damn pill failed? How in the hell could this be happening to me? Murphy again. To top it all off, I could look out of my room and see all kinds of doctors right there. You mean to tell me only one of these jackasses could do it? If I could have moved my hand, I would have thrown something at them all sitting out there.

Thank God for Nurse E. I was so depressed when I found out the pill didn't work. I'm sure she could tell by looking at me. Well, she gave me a shave. I know it seems small, but remember it's the little things that count. I felt semi-human again for a while. She sat with me until I calmed down. She reminded me of all the reasons I had to live. It can be easy to lose sight of the big picture when you let yourself get down. Are you starting to see what a team effort cancer is? I had a great team.

FRIDAY, AUGUST 7, 2009

The squeaky wheel gets a second camera pill...

Dear Family and Friends,

I really think I've missed my calling. I should probably be a patient advocate or hospital administrator or something. After hounding all the doctors yesterday about the camera pill not working and them giving me a story about the GI doctor being on vacation, somehow I got a hold of him, and they set up a new pill for this morning. The doctor said the pill itself was a dud, so I guess the sales representative for the pill gave them a free one. The bottom line is the second pill got inserted this morning about 8:30 a.m. and all is well.

Bob spent his first night last night off the ventilator, and he did fantastic. His blood pressure and heart rate are good. He's just coughing up a heck of a lot of mucus from the yeast infection in his lungs. I'm not going to lie—it's pretty gross and I feel bad for him, but I can see he's back to his old self finally. They are giving him Ativan for the anxiety, and they changed his antibiotics to see if that was affecting his platelet levels.

He's watching ESPN and still can't talk, but he's starting on day two of physical therapy. He has a long road ahead of him, but it looks like he's made it over the hump.

Keep on praying for him. Love and thanks,

— Michele

It's funny reading that Michele suggested she should be a patient advocate. I really do think she should write a book about it. So many things are wrong with the medical industry that you need someone like her fighting for you. Don't get me wrong—the Dr. and Nurse E were great, and I'm alive because of them. But some of those other nurses and doctors didn't give a shit about me. They couldn't care less if I got what I needed.

Oh and squeaky wheel...this means Michele raised holy hell. When she wants to be, she can be your worst nightmare. She wouldn't leave the doctors alone until I got what I needed. She called, complained to the desk, and called again until someone gave her the answers she wanted.

SATURDAY, AUGUST 8, 2009

Look who's talking!

Dear Family and Friends,

Lots of positive things have been happening in the last 24 hours. The camera pill was a success. However, we won't have the results until Monday. Also, Bob got a new valve for his trach, so he's finally able to talk! He sounds very weak and hoarse, but it's something! He has also started physical therapy on his arms and even sat at the edge of the bed on his own. By next week, he should hopefully be eating and moved out of the ICU.

Thanks for all the prayers and support.

Love and thanks,

— Michele

Talk is too strong of a word. I was able to get some audible sounds out, but you still couldn't really understand me. This continued to be a very frustrating condition. I couldn't communicate. Then I got mad at myself and my blood pressure would skyrocket. I had so much I wanted to ask and say. My strength was still wavering and being unable to speak just left me with more questions in my head.

I have to tell you that sitting at the edge of my bed scared the shit out of me. Nurse E came through again and stayed with me through physical therapy. I had learned to trust her, and I knew she wouldn't let anything bad happen to me. I just had this fear that the physical therapist was going to send me tumbling to the floor. All of this was new to me, and all of it scared me. I was trying to learn to sit again at 39 years old. Can you imagine how that feels?

SATURDAY, AUGUST 8, 2009

Here's a photo

Dear Family and Friends,

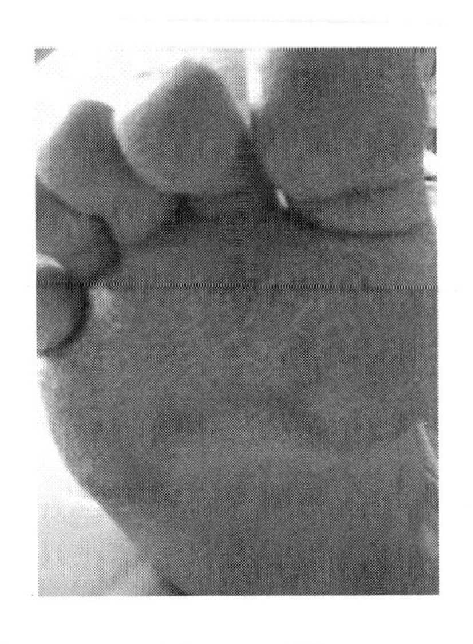

I snuck out for a few hours while Bob was sleeping today to see a movie with my mom. We saw *Julie and Julia*. It got me thinking about this blog I'm writing. However helpful and descriptive it is, it's missing something—photos.

Bob has been adamant that he doesn't want me taking photos of him and posting them and that he isn't ready for visitors yet. But to make everyone happy, I'll compromise. I won't post any photos of Bob's face, but I think most everything else is OK. So today's photo—although gross—is a picture of his foot. He has severe edema, which I've mentioned before, but it's compounded by the worst dry skin I've ever seen. It doesn't help that he hasn't showered in fifty days or walked around. I try to lotion his feet whenever I'm there. He seems to like it because he thinks I'm giving him a foot massage. Whatever works. Let me know if you dig the photos or if they're too much information and I'll stop posting them.

P.S. Although Bob is getting better, he still continues to bleed. Hopefully by Monday we'll have some answers.

Love and thanks,

— Michele

I definitely didn't want anyone to see me. I hadn't seen much of myself, but I knew I looked like crap. I couldn't have weighed more than 185 lbs. To this day, my feet still hurt. I think it's because my feet got wedged in the bottom of the bed, and the night nurses didn't bother to move me. Keep in mind I still wasn't strong enough to move myself anywhere. I remember sitting there at night trying with all my might to move a little, but I didn't get anywhere. I tried over and over and got nowhere.

Yes, I hadn't showered in over fifty days. There wasn't any amount of sponge bathing to help that. You know when you smell so bad you gross yourself out? Well, that's how bad I stunk, except I couldn't move or do anything about it. I just had to lay there and take it. It was one more thing that made me feel less than human. I couldn't even clean myself. It is truly embarrassing and degrading to need someone to clean you. I must admit though that the sponge baths did make me feel better, but it's extremely uncomfortable to strip in front of a stranger to be cleaned.

MONDAY, AUGUST 10, 2009

Green applesauce...the best Bob's ever had

Dear Family and Friends,

As we patiently wait for the results of the camera pill test to hopefully discover where Bob is mysteriously bleeding from, I thought I'd share what happened on Saturday with Bob and the speech therapist.

On Friday, the speech therapist gave Bob a Passy-Muir valve that we can place over his trach. It gives him the ability to speak, though very hoarsely. Nonetheless, he can speak. On Saturday, she came back and told Bob that she was giving him a swallow test to see if food or water would go into his stomach or aspirate into his lungs. Bob's eyes lit up like a kid at Christmas. Due to the soreness of his throat from having the tubes in them for the last three weeks, he's been begging for any type of

water or ice since he's been awake. He's been begging so much so that he's stopped anybody who's walking by and asked for a piece of ice. He'll ask every five minutes for six hours straight, and I joked with him that he reminds me of a drug addict. Anyway, his prayers were answered. The speech therapist walked in with a glass of water and some applesauce and mixed it with green dye so she could see if it came out his trach. He went to town on it, smiling from ear to ear.

My big concern is that Bob still has a severe lung infection. He's been coughing up phlegm so forcefully out of the trach that it has shot across the room and stuck to the far wall (gross but accurate). The pulmonologist's main concern is that if Bob has sugar and it got into his lungs, the fungus that was in there before could start growing again.

As my role as patient advocate, I felt it was my responsibility to tell the speech therapist what the pulmonologist had said. Bob said I was stealing his pleasure of eating. Be that as it may, I'd rather see him alive without a lung infection than him have the instant gratification of green applesauce. So the speech therapist only let Bob have two bites. Bob said the green applesauce was the best he had ever had!

As she expected, he expectorated it into his lungs, and he coughed it out through the trach tube. She said he needed to practice speaking for the rest of the weekend so his lungs and throat get stronger. She said she'd come back later that day and test him again. Needless to say, Bob's new question became, "Is the speech therapist coming back soon?" He asked me that question ten times yesterday!

Bob is alert and was able to have a video conference call with Christopher yesterday. It went very well, and it was fantastic to see him smiling. Just to let everyone know, I started reading everyone's emails to Bob yesterday. Although I might not have time to write everyone back, please know I'm reading all the emails myself as well as all the older ones that everyone sent to Bob. Thank you again for all the kind words.

I'll write again as soon as I hear back from the GI doctor on the source of Bob's bleeding (cross your fingers). If they can't pinpoint it, I'm not really sure what to do next.

Love and thanks,

— Michele

I can still say that green applesauce was the best applesauce I've ever had in my life. I also got a couple sips of apple juice too. Yes, it had green dye in it. It was like heaven on earth to me. I hadn't had anything to eat or drink for longer than I could remember. It tasted so good. Shooting it all out through the trach tube was well worth it. I had green junk all over the wall and a huge smile on my face.

The video conference with Christopher gave me strength. I had to pour all my strength into it, but it was worth it. It took everything I had in me for him to be able to hear me even a little bit, but it meant so much to me to see his face and hear his voice. Afterward, I was so tired from just trying to focus and speak that I passed out for a couple hours.

After coming out of the coma, sleep was a hard commodity to come by. I always had someone coming into my room at all hours of the day and night to take my blood pressure or temperature. Over the next month, I don't think I slept for more than a couple hours at a time. My world became family visits during the day and television at night. I watched SportsCenter *over and over again. When morning came, I could recite it by memory. How bad is that?*

MONDAY, AUGUST 10, 2009

I told them so...

Dear Family and Friends,

I'm very angry right now, so in order to calm myself down, I'm going to talk about the positive things first. Yesterday, they removed the dialysis tube from Bob's neck. Basically, the surgeon just yanked it out when Bob wasn't looking. He wasn't given any anesthesia or anything. Bob did really well. Today, the physical therapist came in and got Bob to actually stand up. He's been sitting in a chair in his room for the last four hours. In addition, the speech therapist came back today and retested Bob with swallowing the green applesauce and water. It was Bob's favorite part of the day, and he did great. There wasn't any aspiration into his lungs. Tomorrow will be the final test. They'll do a video swallow exam and follow the fluids (I guess with a CT scan or something) to ensure they aren't going into his lungs. Bob is very happy, excited, and optimistic today. He's obsessing with food right now, not the bigger picture—that's my obsession.

That being said, here's the part I'm angry about. I had to stalk the GI doctor this morning. I called his office and his nurse, I called the nurse at the hospital, and I had him paged. He was supposed to read Bob's video capsule this morning. He *finally* called me back at 1:30 p.m. and said, "I've got some bad news. The capsule showed that Bob is still actively bleeding." (This is what I've been saying for the past two weeks!) He said the area that's bleeding is lower than the place where they had previously cut. (Remember how mad I was that they didn't look at the rest of the lower fifteen feet of Bob's intestine?!) Well surprise! That's where the bleed is coming from.

I got the doctors to admit two weeks ago that they didn't look at that part because they were sure the part they'd cut out *had* to be the only spot. Then they changed their story and said they couldn't go any further because of risk of perforating the remaining fifteen feet. So if I believe their second story—that they couldn't go any further for risk of perforation—why would I let them try it again? The camera pill showed active bleeding but couldn't determine if it was from a blood vessel, tumor, or ulcer. (I'm hoping ulcer because that's what he's been having.) So now we have to make a decision. Do we let the original GI doctor and surgeon cut him open again, or do we have him transferred to a hospital equipped to do a double balloon endoscopy (the ability to see the whole intestine—all thirty feet)?

To make things worse, I spoke to Bob's oncologist for a long time today. Although Bob is in remission, the course of chemotherapy for leukemia is seven days initially (which he's already had) followed by three days of chemotherapy at a lower dosage on days 30, 60, 90, and 120 to ensure that all the leukemia cells are killed. We've obviously missed day 30 on the schedule. However, the doctor is concerned that if we don't start the three-day therapy soon, the leukemia could come back with a vengeance and it would be much harder to get rid of the second time around. Then Bob would need to start back at the beginning with the stronger seven-day treatment. So it's imperative that we get the three-day chemo started soon. No one wants to do the chemo though because Bob is actively bleeding. So we have to fix the bleeding as soon as possible. That's why I'm so frustrated. We have lots of big decisions to make and they need to be made quickly so we can stop Bob's bleeding and get him started on the three-day chemo. I encourage people to put comments below.

One step forward, two steps back. Please keep Bob in your prayers.

Love and thanks,

— Michele

I didn't do well when they yanked out the dialysis tube. It freaked me out. The doctor didn't give me any warning. He just pulled it out. I thought something was terribly wrong and the tube had just fallen out of my neck. I really wish he would have told me what was going to happen. This particular doctor did things like this again down the road. He wasn't my favorite.

Most everything that happened on this day scared me. Standing was so scary to me. I could barely sit up on my own so standing was a huge deal. I just had this picture in my head of me sprawled out on the floor in a hospital gown screaming, "Help me! I can't get up!"

The green applesauce made the day tolerable. The speech therapist even let me have an ice cube. She was a great lady. My throat was still killing me because the breathing tube had been in there for so long. Yeah, the applesauce was great. Not as good as the first time but still pretty dang good.

My first thought when Michele told me I was still bleeding internally was that I was going to die. I was very depressed and quiet. Michele somehow managed to pick me up and remind me that it was time to fight. I thought back to when my dad had told me it was time to fight. My resolve came back. I would be the one standing in the end. I was reminded of my friend Alwyn's favorite saying—FUCK cancer. Nope, I wasn't going to die now. If I had made it this far, I was going to live. I kept trying to tell myself that over and over again.

There were many decisions to be made, but I was in no shape to make them. Michele tried to explain it all to me, but it was too much for me to deal with. I told her to sort it out and do whatever she thought was best. I told her I would keep fighting. Again, it was my job to fight and her job to make the decisions. Now you can see why I think I would be dead without her. She met with all the doctors and tried to sort through all the information she was getting. I'm sure it must have been overwhelming for her. I didn't mean to put all the pressure of making these potentially life-

threatening decisions on her, but she took charge and made the right decision every time.

TUESDAY, AUGUST 11, 2009

Tentative move to the Cleveland Clinic

Dear Family and Friends,

Today was a very busy day for Bob. I stayed home from work sick, and Bob had his final swallow test. He did pretty well. He is now allowed to eat solid foods and drink thick liquids. He isn't allowed water or Gatorade unless it has a thickening agent in it. No ice cubes either. Bob had Jell-O and half of a hamburger for his first meal. He was glad they took the feeding tube out of his nose.

Now to the bigger picture stuff. I had a long talk with the director of staff, who was also Bob's surgeon and Bob's oncologist. According to the results of the pill endoscopy, Bob is still bleeding, and although the oncologist says it's imperative that we move to start the next round of chemo as soon as possible, she doesn't feel comfortable doing it until he stops bleeding. The surgeon said he didn't feel comfortable operating on Bob a second time and felt Bob might best be served going to a facility with an available double balloon enteroscopy because it is the least invasive next step. They gave me time to sit and talk it over with Bob, and then I called Bob's sister to discuss the situation. We felt that the best choice right now was to keep him as close to home as possible, so we chose to move Bob to the Cleveland Clinic in western Ft. Lauderdale. It's our intention to transfer him there as soon as possible to have the procedure. As soon as he's stopped bleeding, we'll have him transferred back here to finish the chemo. Tomorrow we're going to get the ball rolling so hopefully he can be moved by Thursday. I pray this is the right choice. I feel like it is.

Bob is very scared and rightfully so. He has another battle to fight. Please keep him in your thoughts and prayers.

P.S. They did an x-ray today on Bob's stomach. Both camera pills are stuck, so they had to give him milk of magnesia and stool softeners in order to move them along. Hopefully he'll pass them tonight.

Love and thanks,

— Michele

Finally I could eat and sort of drink. Anything I drank had to be "thickened" with a small pack of what looked like Jell-O mix. My only problem was my stomach wasn't used to actual food, so I could only eat a little bit at a time. This really sucked because I wanted so badly to chow down. But after a little bit, the nausea hit. Oh did it ever hit!

That hamburger was incredible. I finally felt like I was taking some steps forward instead of moving backward all the time. The feeding tube hurt like hell coming out, but it meant I could finally see my son for real. I didn't want him to see me with tubes everywhere. I think seeing a tube in my nose up close would have scared him too much.

The "brain trust" had a decision to make. They decided it would be best for me to go to the Cleveland Clinic in Ft. Lauderdale. I was cool with that if it was what they thought was best.

The camera pill thing doesn't sound big, but when you don't have the strength to make it to the bathroom, milk of magnesia and stool softeners are a nightmare. I can say one of the most degrading things I had to do was crap in a plastic urinal. It doesn't get much worse than needing someone to wipe your butt because you don't have the strength to do it yourself. And you're laying in your own bed while it's happening. I felt less than human again.

THURSDAY, AUGUST 13, 2009

Both camera pills are out, and Bob is moving to the Cleveland Clinic today

Dear Family and Friends,

I'm sorry I didn't have a chance to update the blog yesterday, but I had to work and make a million phone calls to set up Bob's move to the Cleveland Clinic. Basically we are on standby until we get a phone call from the Cleveland Clinic letting us know a bed has opened in their ICU. They said once the doctors make their rounds this morning, they will probably downgrade someone and Bob will be able to go. He wants me to ride in the ambulance with him, so as soon as I get the call, I'm going to leave work and head over to Bethesda.

As you can see from the picture, Bob has finally passed the two camera pills that were hanging out in his stomach for the past week. They had given him some stool softeners and milk of magnesia and they came out. Unfortunately, passing the camera pills combined with Bob eating regular food has caused him to go from slowly oozing blood to bleeding again. His platelets dropped last night to 77,000. (Two weeks ago they were at 350,000.)

Now for some great news. Bob was able to see his son Christopher yesterday. He was able to sit right next to him and talk with him. According to Christopher's grandmother, he was with Bob for about thirty minutes. I went over to her house and ate dinner with Chris and asked him about seeing his dad. He said, "It was good. Dad looks the same, just skinnier." So it was great that he wasn't afraid. I think that was the best motivation for Bob to get better.

Last night I was able to speak to the new GI doctor, who will be taking care of Bob's intestinal bleeding. He called me at about 6:45 p.m., and we spoke for about thirty minutes. He was very open-minded and honest with me about Bob's condition, and we talked about options for Bob. They hope to evaluate him today and possibly do the double balloon enteroscopy tomorrow or perform surgery.

If you want me to be detailed, here it is—our first option is the double balloon enteroscopy. It doesn't require Bob to be cut open. It involves an inflated balloon that pushes against the wall of the intestine as it slinks itself downward. The problem is that Bob just had the first surgery only three weeks ago. If the balloon passes through the part where they cut and sewed, there is a chance the area isn't completely healed and the balloon could rupture it. They usually wait 6–8 weeks before performing this procedure.

The other option is surgery. From what I understand, they would open Bob back up, cut him where they did before, stick the camera directly into the intestine, look all the way down to the bottom this time (unlike in his last surgery), fix and cut whatever they needed to, and sew him back up. His bleeding would stop for good then.

A little bit about Bob's new doctor...subsequent to his current appointment, he was regional chief of gastroenterology at Kaiser Permanente, Ohio. After receiving his bachelor's of medicine/bachelor's of surgery in 1990, he completed his residency at the Cleveland Clinic. His research and clinical interests include general gastroenterology, capsule endoscopy, double balloon enteroscopy, obscure GI bleeding, diagnostic and therapeutic endoscopy, and diseases of the small bowel. He is the recipient of an array of academic awards, including the Dr. Sidney Garfield Physician of Excellence Award, a teaching award presented by the internal medicine residents at Case Western Reserve University Hospital in Cleveland, Ohio, and an Outstanding Senior Medical Resident Award from the Cleveland Clinic. So it sounds like Bob's in good hands.

OK—back to Bob being transferred. The only way Bob was willing to go to the Cleveland Clinic was if he could go back to Bethesda for chemo. He wanted to be close to home and I can understand that. So yesterday Bethesda signed a letter of reciprocity (which I made sure to get a copy of) stating that Bob is going to the Cleveland Clinic to be treated for GI issues only and that once he is stable Bethesda will have 48 hours to take him back, provided they have a bed for him. That's all the news that's fit to print right now. Just waiting.

If I could say thank you to anyone today, it would be to Bob's nurse, Nurse E. I really don't know how Bob or I would have pulled through this without her kindness. Let me tell you I had to pull some strings to have her put on Bob's case full-time, but she has made all the difference. It's amazing how going the extra mile can change someone's life for the better. Saying thank you doesn't even begin to cover it.

Please keep Bob in your prayers, and thanks to everyone for the opinions they've been posting. I read them all!

Lots of love and thanks,

— Michele

I finally crapped out the pills. Thank you for small miracles. I couldn't take much more milk of magnesia. I was scared again because the bleeding seemed to be back with a vengeance. It just wouldn't stop. At this point, it was obvious to me that I needed to get to the Cleveland Clinic and get this fixed. I couldn't shake the thought that I was going to bleed to death.

The visit from Christopher was great. It had been a while since I had seen him and I needed it. During chemo, it doesn't matter how many times you tell yourself you're going to be OK. You need to draw strength from others. I sucked up all the strength my family had. I think at this point everyone was starting to break down. They were giving me all they had and it didn't seem to be enough. I was hanging in there, but the rough times were far from over. How much could they continue to give?

I didn't get all the medical stuff. I still left it all to Michele to deal with. I didn't understand or care to understand. I just wanted to get better. I also knew I wouldn't make it through this if I didn't have my family around me. So I emphatically insisted that I come back to Bethesda. I knew I could count on the daily visits from my mom and dad, and I knew Christopher would be there a couple of days per week. I also knew Michele could go home and get a little bit of rest away from me and my ordeal.

I need to make a special thank you to my ex-wife, Sarah. She was very understanding when it came to bringing Christopher in to see me. I think she knew I needed to see him. She was a huge help when she didn't have to be. Thank you.

Nurse E is amazing. I remember her sitting with me and holding my hand after Christopher left because I couldn't stop crying. She gave me all the strength she had as well. I can never put into words how much she meant to me. I must say that 99 percent of the nurses who helped me were great. There were a couple not so good ones. They may have just been having a bad day or something, but the nurses at Bethesda were great! Nurse E is tied for number one with another nurse you'll get to meet later.

The move had me nervous. Was this the right decision? Would the move end up killing me or saving me? What quality of care would I get? I had so many questions and not many answers.

FRIDAY, AUGUST 14, 2009

So long for now Bethesda, hello Cleveland Clinic

Dear Family and Friends,

After waiting until 11:00 p.m. last night to be transferred, Bob finally made it to the Cleveland Clinic in Weston. I followed behind the ambulance in my car. The EMT actually knew one of Bob's friends (Charlie), so it made for a smoother ride for Bob.

After getting here, I was amazed at how spacious the room was (it looks like Bob's staying in a hotel room) and how welcoming the night nurse was. She offered Bob some food and Jell-O and gave me a bed in Bob's room to sleep in, and we were seen by two of the internists. I gave them the rundown of everything Bob had and they took blood, and we slept until morning. I'd give our night nurse, Laura, a solid B+.

Morning came and we got a new nurse—a guy named Patrick who seemed to be in training. Patrick got a "D" for Bob's care. I didn't want to come out with guns blazing today so that I'd get a reputation for being a pain, but every time Bob needed something, I had to ask three times. The internal medicine team rounded this morning, and I went over all of Bob's records again. My biggest concern was that Bob is getting *none* of the medicine he was getting at Bethesda. He's not getting any Protonix for ulcers or blood pressure medicine. Nothing. I told just about everyone who came in the room, and twelve hours later nothing had changed. I told them Bob needed a special air bed for the wound on his butt. It has gone down to the fat layer. Even though the night nurse ordered it last night (it's 8:00 p.m. now on the next day), Bob still hasn't received it. Patrick, his nurse, told us the beds are outsourced by a separate company and that it could take up to 24 hours.

Speaking of wound care, I told them yesterday that Bob needed to be seen by a wound care specialist. No one came by and I asked three times, so the nurses changed it. I harassed them as much as I could, but they said he'd have to wait until tomorrow. In addition, Bob had to have a CT scan of his abdomen done today. When he got back at 1:00 p.m., he was starving. They didn't get him lunch. I had to ask Patrick three times to order it and it took two hours. Although this is a very high-tech hospital with really nice rooms, I don't see the personalized care he had at Bethesda. I'm hoping I'm wrong, but we'll see.

More importantly, the GI doctors stopped by. Bethesda didn't send over all the records, so I had to spend the morning getting them to fax pathology GI reports over here. Trust me—if I didn't do it, it wouldn't have been done until next week. The GI doctors didn't want to make any decisions about how to proceed with Bob until they received all the records. So at around 3:00 p.m., they came by and we discussed it. Unfortunately, they said the pathology report was vague, so they need to request the actual slides from Bethesda.

This will probably take until Monday. Their pathologist has to read the slides and then they will decide how to proceed. So Bob most likely won't be having surgery until the middle of next week. The good news is the GI doctors were really nice. They had their act together, and they explained why they needed the pathology report and slides to make the best decision about Bob. That being said, they understood the need to stop the bleeding as quickly as possible in order for Bob to receive the consolidation therapy. Speaking of chemo, the oncologist came by and he was very nice. One strange thing he said was that this hospital doesn't have a dedicated oncology ward.

Bob's new night nurse just came in. Let's hope she's better than the day nurse. Hopefully, she can get Bob his new bed. Keep your fingers crossed!

Love and thanks,

— Michele

As Michele said, one of the EMT guys knew my buddy Charlie Fay, so he took great care of me. We shared some stories about Charlie, which helped pass the time. The ambulance ride was misery. My butt was still pretty much chewed up hamburger. I had the mother of all bedsores. Every bump we hit felt like I was getting smacked on the butt with a paddle.

So the first day didn't go so well. All I ask from my nurses is that they get me my pain medicines on time so I don't have to be in any more agony than necessary. When that doesn't happen, I get pretty pissed. Chemo and cancer are all about taking the pain. Today I was in a lot of it.

SATURDAY, AUGUST 15, 2009

Third camera pill, Monday morning

Dear Family and Friends,

After speaking with the GI doctors this morning, they determined that while they are waiting for the pathology slides to come from Bethesda, they are going to repeat the camera pill to be on the safe side. They want to make sure Bob is still bleeding enough to warrant surgery. Bob and I were both happy they were being so proactive.

Today was a much better day with the nurses too. The nurse has been giving Bob his pain medication on every even hour without having to be reminded (this is a huge plus in Bob's book). We finally got his air mattress delivered today (I had to call the nursing supervisor and it was delivered in ten minutes), and Bob started physical therapy. The woman kicked his butt. Today was the first day that Bob stood up and did exercises (holding on to the back of a chair). One of them was squatting. He could only squat three inches from knees locked (so hardly at all), but it's a start. (It was very hard for me to not start yelling, "Back, back, back...up!" But I thought he'd get mad.)

Anyhow, now we're waiting for the wound care nurse. That's the only person who hasn't come yet. I hope she comes soon.

They have decided to take Bob off all antibiotics and antifungals today. Please keep Bob in your prayers. Thanks again for all the kind words of support.

Love and thanks,

— Michele

Like I said, just get me my pain meds on time and I'm a happy camper. Physical therapy kicked my butt. When you're going through chemo and cancer, all you want to do is rest. It did feel good mentally to get up and move around a bit. It was another small step to feeling like I was moving forward.

The squats hurt a lot because my butt was so torn up. I paid for it later because my butt bled like crazy. Michele's joke about "back" and "up" is from powerlifting. In order for a lifter to get a legal squat, he needs to squat down to a certain depth. The coach will call you down by saying, "Back, back, back...up." I probably would have laughed my sore butt off if she had said it.

MONDAY, AUGUST 17, 2009

My birthday wish...

Dear Family and Friends,

As most of you know, today is my 35th birthday. (Thanks, by the way, for all the phone calls and emails!) I spent yesterday with my family, which was nice, and my mom and dad as well as Bob's parents came down to the Cleveland Clinic to see Bob. I think that made him very happy. Today they're doing the camera pill, and it's really amazing to see how much Bob improves day by day. My biggest birthday present was Dave Tate from EliteFTS.com coming down late last night. He is one of Bob's closest friends, and he's going to watch over the nurses while I'm at work this week. That's going to be a huge help!

Bob's big PR yesterday was that he walked the length of the room without the nurse's help and only the use of a walker. His physical therapy is getting better each time he does it. Now he has Dave to work with him as well. We're still waiting on the wound

Photo credit: willheffernan

care nurse to come and look at the gaping wound on Bob's backside. They promised me this morning that they'd get on it. If they don't, they'll have Dave to contend with!

I'll update more when I find out the results of the camera pill and the slides from pathology. Then we'll know how they're going to proceed with the bleeding.

Love and thanks,

— Michele

Dave is like a brother to me. We have been through the highs and lows of each other's lives for fifteen years. Here is what Dave posted on his website when he first heard I was sick:

> *For those of you who have been readers of this site over the years, you'll know that Bob Youngs was the very first person I brought on the Q & A to help me out. Over the years, his passion for helping others with their training has been demonstrated by the articles and thousands of Q & As he has written and answered. No question was ever too small for Bob to answer. He was one of the first to answer, "What do you do if you don't have a reverse hyper?" and was still around to answer it again for the 500th time.*

> *As some of you may know, though I'm sure many more don't, Bob was just diagnosed with acute myeloid leukemia and started chemotherapy yesterday.*
>
> *Bob is a very dear friend of mine and has been there for me in many ways over the years. There isn't any way for me to express the impact he has had on EliteFTS, other team members, my family, and me. To do so would not do him the justice he deserves. I know for a fact that one person can make a difference. He did for me and will continue to do so.*
>
> *Bob is also among the strongest people I know when it comes to overcoming adversity, so there isn't any doubt in my mind that he will beat this, but he will be in my prayers nonetheless.*

Dave couldn't have come at a better time. Michele needed help, and I needed help. We both needed someone else to draw strength from, and Dave delivered. He and I spent hours watching CSI *and other daytime television shows. When I needed someone to carry me to the bathroom, he did it. When I needed food, he got it. I think we all just needed him there at that time. There aren't many people in the world you can count on like that. I'm glad now that I had both Michele and Dave.*

TUESDAY, AUGUST 18, 2009

Camera pill postponed until today

Dear Family and Friends,

I know you must be sick of me talking about all these camera pills, but they postponed this until today. According to Dave, Bob was actually going to have to swallow two of them and sit upright in a chair for eleven hours. Bob hadn't seen the wound care specialist yet, so they decided to wait until today. Wound care finally came at 7:30 p.m. last night. They put a Duoderm patch on Bob's wound and determined that he has a "stage 3 wound," which means it's eaten through all the skin and has exposed fat. Trust me—my heart goes out to Bob. It looks like it hurts. I can only imagine how it feels. Also, yesterday they took the catheter out of Bob, which is good, and both Dave and the physical therapists had him up and walking with the walker.

They are bringing Bob down to the endoscopy area around 3:00 p.m., so I'll report once we hear more. Bob's parents are also coming down because Bob has requested that his mom make him some spaghetti. At least his appetite is coming back!

As always, thanks for keeping Bob in your thoughts and prayers.

Love and thanks,

— Michele

I knew I needed the camera pill and I knew I needed to stop bleeding, but they wanted me to sit up in a chair for eleven hours? I told the doctor he could look at my butt if he wanted, but there wasn't any way I could sit in a chair for eleven hours. My butt was in bad shape. How was I going to sit up for that long?

I had been craving my mom's spaghetti for about a month. Can you imagine how much you crave something when you've been thinking about eating it for a month? Well, my parents got there, and the doctors decided to bring me down for the pill procedure early. In all the time I spent in hospitals, this was the only time I think anything was done early. So no spaghetti for me, but it sure did look good.

TUESDAY, AUGUST 18, 2009

Bob rushed to ICU, coughing blood

Dear Family and Friends,

Bob had a big scare today after they inserted the camera pill. His blood pressure dropped to 70/35, and his heart rate skyrocketed. They think it could have been from the Propophyl—the same drug that killed Michael Jackson. Then Bob started coughing up blood. They had to move him to the surgical ICU unit. They won't let me stay with him, so I'm at the hotel. When we left, his blood pressure was stable at 118/64, and his heart rate was at 118. He is still coughing up lots of blood, and they don't know the cause. They did two chest x-rays and will do a CT scan of his stomach in a few hours. I'll update everyone in the morning.

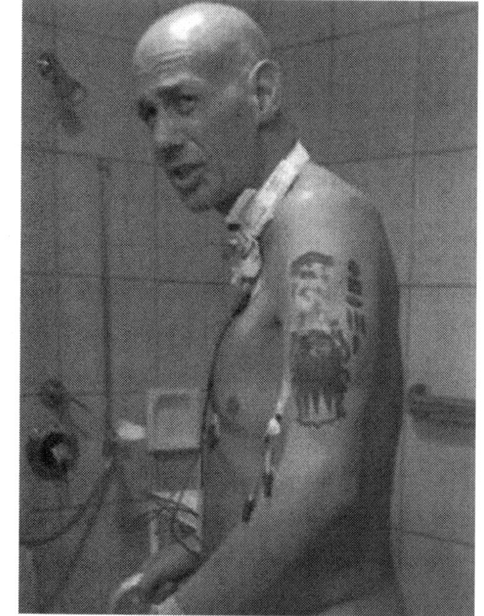

Bob needs lots of prayers tonight.

Love and thanks,

— Michele

This was the one time everyone got all worked up and I actually knew I was OK. They had changed my trach tube earlier in the day and it had cut up my throat. I knew that's what it was. I don't know how I knew, but I did. However, I was pissed. When my blood pressure dropped, the nurses all freaked out, and they were trying to give me an IV. The nurse missed a vein five times. I'm not exaggerating. I told the nurse that if she missed again, I was going to jump up off the table and stick her with the needle. They brought in another nurse who got it on the first try.

The ICU nurse was great. I think somehow she could tell by my behavior that I was OK. I also couldn't sleep. She came in to give me my pain meds (if you can't tell by now, that's when I was the happiest) and asked if she could do something nice for me. She said all her other patients were asleep. So I said, "Something nice would be great." She told me not to go anywhere (she had a great sense of humor) and that she'd be right back. She came back and shaved my face for me. That one little thing made me feel like a new man. I still couldn't sleep, and I was on my fifth rerun of SportsCenter, *but I was smiling.*

WEDNESDAY, AUGUST 19, 2009

Very frustrated...

Dear Family and Friends,

Bob is still in the ICU. I just got through speaking with the GI doctor regarding the camera pill, and another snag happened. Apparently, the camera pill cut off right after it went through the area where Bob had previously had his intestines reattached. (Ten days ago, we confirmed with the second camera pill that Bob wasn't bleeding at that site.) This pill reconfirmed what we already knew but was unable to address if Bob was still bleeding a few feet below the site, which was the whole reason we came to the Cleveland Clinic. I expressed my frustration to the doctor and again explained the importance of something happening with regards to the GI bleed so that Bob can have his second round of chemotherapy. The doctor assured me that he was going to consult with the rest of the GI doctors and that they would make a decision today about whether or not they would proceed with the double balloon enteroscopy or move to operate. In the meanwhile, Bob continues to cough up blood but far less than yesterday. They are monitoring the situation closely.

Please keep Bob in your thoughts and prayers.

Love and thanks,

— Michele

I don't know what it was, but somehow I felt better mentally. The physical pain was still there, but I knew that everything was going to be OK. Yes, I was upset the camera pill didn't work, but for some reason, I was more at peace. I have no explanation for it.

THURSDAY, AUGUST 20, 2009

Decision time

Dear Family and Friends,

I spoke with the GI doctor this morning regarding the unsuccessfulness of the third camera pill. They are going to be reviewing the pathology slides, the results from the second camera pill that worked, and all of Bob's blood work over the past week to make a determination as to whether they want to proceed with the double balloon endoscopy or whether they believe Bob has stopped bleeding. If they believe Bob has stopped bleeding, they will release him back to Bethesda tomorrow. At this point, I told them that whatever it is, they need to decide today because we've already lost a week, which could have been used for giving him chemotherapy. The GI doctor said he would call me back later today with a decision. In the meanwhile, Bob continues to cough up blood, although it is much less than yesterday. I

will continue to follow up today with them until a decision has been made and let everyone know.

P.S. Here is a photo of the team that hosted the "Pulling for Bob" powerlifting event last week. Again, special thanks to both the World Gym Power Performance team of Ft. Meyers and Southside Barbell. Thanks to all!

Love and thanks,

— Michele

Dave and I spent the day reminiscing about our old days—long rides to powerlifting meets and all the stupid stuff that had happened in the gym or to people we knew. Somehow Dave managed to keep my mind off everything else going wrong around me. I'm sure he knew I just wasn't up for dealing with all the medical emergencies going on. For me, it was just a day spent with an old friend remembering all the fun stuff we had done together.

The double balloon endoscopy was a scary thought for me. They were concerned the procedure might kill me, but if I continued to bleed, I was going to die. I was in a "damned if I do and damned if I don't" situation. I really felt like we were getting nowhere. Had this trip been a waste?

FRIDAY, AUGUST 21, 2009

Bob going back to Bethesda hospital today...

Dear Family and Friends,

Lots of news since the last blog. After speaking with the GI doctors from the Cleveland Clinic, it is their belief that Bob is no longer bleeding from his small bowel. After reading the pathology slides from the surgery, they determined that Bob had small bowel ischemia where there is a loss of blood to the intestine. They felt the ulcer could have been caused by the leukemia or the overuse of NSAIDS. They didn't feel a double balloon enteroscopy would be beneficial to Bob at this time. They felt it would do more harm than good and felt comfortable that he could successfully undergo chemotherapy.

That being said, we spoke to both oncologists at the Cleveland Clinic and at Bethesda. They both agreed that because the doctor at Bethesda had all of Bob's records and had completed the initial bone marrow aspirations, Bob's chemo should be continued at Bethesda. When the results come in, we'll take it from there. If he's still in remission and only needs the three-day consolidation therapy, we'll see if he wants to stay at Bethesda or go to Moffett center in Tampa. If he has relapsed (which is a possibility because he has missed his second scheduled chemo by thirty days), we definitely wouldn't keep him at Bethesda. He would go directly to

Tampa for treatment. (Bob has decided to stay in state and not be transferred to Boston as we had originally intended.)

As Bob's friend, Dave, reminded me, this week hasn't been a loss. Bob can now walk with the aid of a walker, he has full mobility of his hands to the point where he texted me this morning, he can speak much more clearly than before with the aid of a Passy-Muir valve, he can use the bathroom, and he is getting stronger. This will continue to be our focus this week as we prepare for the chemo treatments that he has ahead of him.

Thanks to everyone for their continued thoughts, prayers, and support.

Love and thanks,

— Michele

After a lot of hoopla, I stopped bleeding on my own. I wanted to get back to Bethesda. It had become my "home" for the time being. The Dr. was there and I wanted her as my oncologist. What Michele doesn't come out and say is that no one believed there was a shot in hell I was still in remission. My blood counts were a mess, and all signs showed I needed a transplant. I was almost 100 percent sure I was going to have to head to Tampa. I was dreading that, as it was still so far away from my support system. I also knew that if the leukemia was back, my chances of living weren't good.

The little victories added up that week. I could use a walker, and my hands actually did what I wanted them to. The trach valve sucked, but it beat not being able to talk at all. The tube itself helped me pass the time. I could take a Q-tip and clean out all the crap I was spitting out. Anything to help pass the time.

Dave headed back to Ohio. I think we both knew he would be back. I think he saw that I needed him, and more importantly, Michele needed him. I think she had hit rock bottom. The bad news continued to mount, and the fight just seemed to be starting. She and I had taken our fair share of shots to the face, and the fight was headed uphill, but we fought on. There wasn't any other alternative.

SUNDAY, AUGUST 23, 2009

Sunday afternoon update

Dear Family and Friends,

Bob is adjusting very well back at Bethesda. We've had tons of nurses, both from the cancer wing as well as from the ICU, come by to welcome him back. (He's a very popular guy!) Bob is getting stronger every day. He's walking around the room with the help of the walker and setting daily goals. The oncologist confirmed that he isn't bleeding in his stool, which was fantastic, and they feel Bob is strong enough to have the trach out as early as tomorrow. They were unable to perform the bone marrow aspiration on Friday, so Bob's doctor is going to do that first thing tomorrow morning. Bob is also eating like a horse, which is great! We'll know more about what is going on by Wednesday as to whether he is going to stay here for treatment or go elsewhere.

I'll keep everyone posted.

Love and thanks,

— Michele

The good nurses—and Bethesda is loaded with them—really care, so they were happy to see me back. Nurse E sneaked up on her break to say hello and check in on me. Her smile alone added to my resolve. I told her how scared I was about the bone marrow aspiration, and she said it would be fine.

Nurse T was my nurse when I returned to oncology. Nurse T is a leukemia survivor. He was diagnosed when he was in college. He went through treatment at Bethesda, changed his major after he healed up, and became a nurse. Every time he was working, Nurse T seemed to get me as a patient. I think he liked me, and I sure liked having him around. He told it like it was and had been where I wanted to go. He had also been my mom's nurse as well, so we had kind of a history.

All the nurses in oncology were good. They really were. I was glad to be "home." I felt a certain comfort level at Bethesda. My reception from all the nurses really helped pump me up. They had all been with me through my previous medical issues as my primary care providers, and they were really happy to see me alive and making progress.

MONDAY, AUGUST 24, 2009

Bone marrow aspiration completed

Dear Family and Friends,

I stayed at the hospital with Bob last night because the oncologist said she was going to perform the bone marrow aspiration at 6:45 a.m. this morning. She gave Bob Ativan and Demerol to help with the pain and anxiety. He did fantastic. We're now waiting for the pulmonologist to see if Bob's going to get the trach out. I'll let you know as soon as we hear something.

Love and thanks,

— Michele

The Dr. gave me a lot of drugs. Thank God. I think I actually passed out during parts of the bone marrow aspiration. It still hurt like hell, but the drugs made it tolerable. However, when the drugs wore off, the pain was brutal, and there wasn't any way I could sit or lay to make it feel better.

Everyone had a different look on his face during the bone marrow aspiration. I really think the Dr. and all the staff thought the cancer was back due to my blood counts. Things looked really bleak. I just tried to watch television and let the time pass. I think I got hooked on NCIS. *In the back of my mind, I was convinced the leukemia was back. What the hell was I going to have to go through now?*

TUESDAY, AUGUST 25, 2009

Tracheotomy removed; Bob needed blood again...

Dear Family and Friends,

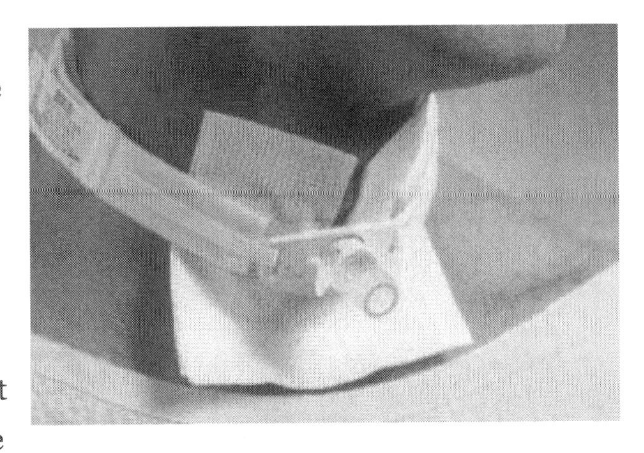

Yesterday Bob's blood results came back, and they were low, which was very concerning for the doctor, especially because Bob hasn't been bleeding. She said it may be an indication his leukemia has returned. We won't know those results for sure until late Wednesday. Hopefully, she's wrong. In the meantime, she had to give Bob two units of packed red blood. His counts were in the 7s. In addition, Bob had his tracheotomy removed. He said it didn't hurt a bit. The only thing is that his throat is very sore, and he can't speak again temporarily because it hurts too much. He has his swallow test later on this afternoon, which he's looking forward to. If he passes, he can drink clear liquids again.

Please say a prayer for Bob in hopes that his leukemia hasn't returned. If it has, he's going to have to be transferred to a specialty cancer hospital possibly out of state, and he's going to have a long road to battle—worse than before (if that's possible).

Love and thanks,

— Michele

The blood results really scared me because it wasn't a good sign. Things weren't looking good, and I thought I would be heading to Tampa soon. I started thinking about a six-hour ride in an ambulance and how my torn up butt would take that.

The same doctor who took out my dialysis unit took out my trach. Again, he just yanked it out and didn't say anything. My blood pressure went from 140/100 to 180/130. It scared the hell out of me. I was really beginning to dislike him. I much preferred knowing what was going to happen first. Then he just laughed like it was funny. If I could have caught him on my walker, I would have beaten his ass.

I passed the swallow test and was allowed liquids. It had been two months since I had had actual liquids. Previously, I could drink, but it had to be thickened. I started off with some Gatorade and PowerAde. It tasted so good. The walker got a lot of use that night because I had to pee so many times, but I was going to enjoy drinking again. Can you imagine how much you want to drink after not having liquid for months?

WEDNESDAY, AUGUST 26, 2009

Miracles exist! Bob is still in remission!!

Dear Family and Friends,

I received a phone call from Bob's oncologist this afternoon. Bob had me on speaker when she came into his room to deliver the news. She said that she spoke to the pathologist this afternoon regarding Bob's prognosis and that miraculously Bob is still in complete remission. They classify remission as less than 5 percent blast cells in the body, and initial reports indicate that Bob has less than 2 percent. The doctor was very surprised, as was I, because all indications in his blood work (the drop in hemoglobin, platelets, and white cells) are indicative of the cancer returning. She had no explanation for it. Bob will still need to receive three-day consolidation chemotherapy, which is still very risky due to his condition, but it won't require him to be transferred to Boston. He and I will be discussing whether or not he wants to remain at Bethesda for continued treatment or possibly go to UM Sylvester in Miami. Either way, they want to start the chemotherapy this week.

In other news, Bob took a barium swallow test to see if he could stop drinking thick liquids and move back to regular liquids like water. He has to drink barium and then they do x-rays to see if the liquid passes to his stomach or if some gets aspirated into his lungs. He passed with flying colors! Good news abounds!

Finally, I'd like to thank everyone again for all the donations. A special thank you goes to Mussa Mohkami, a powerlifter from Germany, for writing Bob a letter today. Although Bob has never met Mussa, his letter was very inspirational. I read it to him this morning when he woke up.

Here's an excerpt:

> *"I do believe in a higher power, a power that is bigger than man. The mind is a great tool—it can make the impossible possible. I believe when you think positive and put all your energy and the energy of friends and family, loved ones, fans, and iron brothers all around the globe together there is nothing you can't do!"*

I echo his sentiments exactly. Thank you to everyone who has been pulling for Bob. It means more than you'll ever know.

Love and thanks,

— Michele

The Dr. walked into the room and was very solemn. I just knew she was going to tell me the leukemia was back again. When she told me I was still in remission, I was in shock. It didn't register at first. The first words out of my mouth were, "Are you shitting me?" The Dr. just grinned and said no. We talked about consolidation therapy, but I don't remember any of it. I finally got a big win. I finally connected with my own punches. I wanted to jump up on the bed and scream.

After the Dr. left, I cried again, but they were tears of joy for the first time in months. I was going to make it! I could do this. I was still in the fight, and it was time to get it on. I needed this. I really did. My hope was wavering, and I needed a win. I had convinced myself that I wasn't in remission. I was really thinking I was facing a battle I couldn't win, or if I did, the win would be short-lived after a transplant.

I also knew the little battles were still the key. Mussa was my little win for the day. When you have nothing to do but sit in bed, you think. You think a lot. I thought about someone taking the time to write me, someone who had never met me and lived in another country. The kindness of so many people gave me strength. I needed them to keep it coming. I had just won a round in the fight, but it wasn't anywhere near over.

THURSDAY, AUGUST 27, 2009

Bob to be transferred to University of Miami cancer center

Dear Family and Friends,

After speaking with Bob and his oncologist last night, Bob feels it would be in his best interests to be transferred to the University of Miami Sylvester Cancer Center. I have been making phone calls, and hopefully, we can get him transferred by tomorrow so that he can start chemotherapy. Everything else is going pretty well. Bob is in good spirits after learning his cancer hasn't come back.

I will write later when I have more to report.

Love and thanks,

— Michele

I had to have a serious talk with the Dr. again. It was just her and me. I felt a special bond with her, and I felt like I was betraying her by looking at other hospitals. I explained to her that it had nothing to do with her or anyone in oncology. I was worried that if I started to bleed again, I wouldn't get the care I needed. The Dr. understood and she was great about it.

SATURDAY, AUGUST 29, 2009

R.I.P. Renegade, 1998–2009

Dear Family and Friends,

Yesterday was a very sad day for our family. My sister's dog, Renegade, had to be put to sleep. He was eleven. Although he was my sister's dog, my whole family felt like he was all of ours. I remember when they brought Ren to my parent's house for the first time. He was such a cute puppy! He tried to bite my toe, and when he ran, he always fell over because his head was so darn big! He reminded me a lot of the movie *Marley and Me*. He was a big, dumb dog who did stupid things sometimes, but we all loved him nonetheless. He never bit anyone but could possibly lick you to death.

My dad loved Renegade most of all. He'd go over to Lori and Tony's house with a pocket full of dog treats, and Ren would drool all over the place. My dad would hide the treats throughout their house so Ren could find them.

Renegade was 125 lbs and died due to complications from hip dysplasia on his hind legs. Renegade was a great dog, and we are all going to miss him.

I know this blog is about Bob's recovery, and I'll write about that next, but I needed to say this about Renegade. With everything that's been going on, the loss of him really affected me yesterday.

Love and thanks,

— Michele

I think Renegade's passing was a big kick in all of our butts that life is finite. While things were improving, people still died. It was a reminder that we couldn't let our guard down. The fight was still on. I knew I could be joining Renegade with one more bad turn. I thought a lot about that. The thought of death is always there. How do you avoid thinking about it?

SATURDAY, AUGUST 29, 2009

Still waiting on transfer...

Dear Family and Friends,

I have been very frustrated with UM and Bob's transfer. We are still waiting on a bed for him at Jackson Memorial, and they aren't too friendly in the admitting department there. I really hope we're making the right decision with regards to transferring him.

For the good news, Bob is getting around so much better! He is now able to walk with a cane and use the restroom on his own. It is definitely giant strides from two weeks ago when he could barely lift his hands. We are working on trying to put some weight on him now.

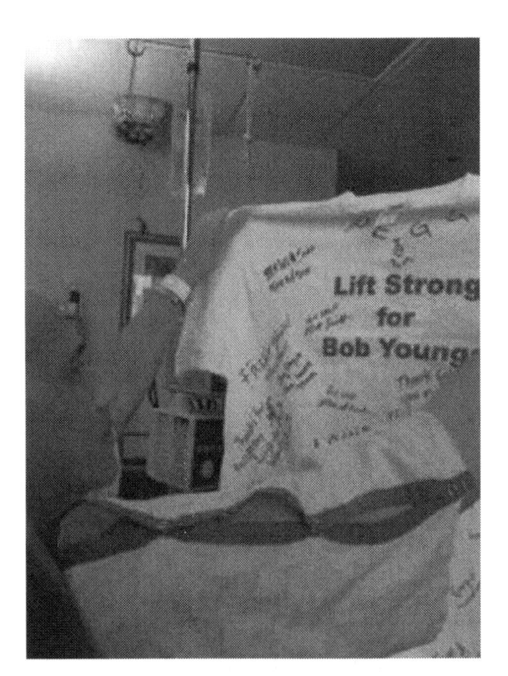

Also, I bought Bob a belated birthday gift. He got a Blackberry, so he's able to read his email again (at least temporarily until the chemo starts), and he also has access to his Facebook page.

Finally, I'd like to say a big thank you to Mike "Paper"

Stuchiner. He participated in the IPA Power Station Pro-Am last weekend and wore a shirt that said "Lift Strong for Bob Youngs." I just received one of them in the mail. He had all of Bob's powerlifting friends sign it. I'm going to give it to Bob today and hang it on his wall in the hospital. I really think it's going to make him happy and lift his spirits.

I promise I'll write more when we get to Miami. Bob's friend Dave is coming on Sunday to help me, and I know we'll have a lot to write about.

Love and thanks,

— Michele

I was starting to get around pretty well, but I knew I needed to get the chemo going and the last round damn near killed me. The good news was that Dave would be back soon. Also, my friend Mike sending me that shirt really made me feel good. It was also the first picture I let Michelle put on the blog that partially showed my face. That was a big step for me.

I didn't want people to see how bad I looked. That wasn't the picture I wanted in people's minds if I died. I wanted to be remembered from the good times we had together. How do you want people to remember you?

MONDAY, AUGUST 31, 2009

Bob to stay in Boynton Beach...

Dear Family and Friends,

After days of fighting with the University of Miami/Jackson over trying to find a bed at their hospital so Bob can receive his chemotherapy, which is 55 days overdue, they finally called this morning to tell me they had a bed for him. Upon further investigation, however, they decided Bob would have to share a room. I reminded them that Bob needed chemo, would be neutropenic soon, and had MRSA. They basically told me "too bad" and that it was a double room or nothing. In addition, I wouldn't be able to spend the night with him either. I asked about the special air mattress that Bob had been using because of his bedsore wound, and they blew me off on that too.

After relaying this to Bob, he'd had about enough. He decided he was going to stay at Bethesda. Although the doctors may not round 24/7 and they aren't on the cutting edge of technology, they do know him as a person and treat him like he matters. Because he's been there for two months, all the nurses know him. They have a vested interest in keeping him alive. They kept him alive the first time when his liver, kidneys, and lungs shut down and he was bleeding internally. I'm satisfied they can do it a second time with the next round of chemotherapy too. The only way we would transfer him is if he needed a transplant, and he isn't at that stage right now.

I spoke with Bob's oncologist, and they are starting the chemo today at 6:00 p.m. Please say a prayer or wish him luck.

Love and thanks,

— Michele

Hindsight is 20/20 and not going to Miami was the best thing for me. I could remain close to my family. More importantly, the doctors and nurses at Bethesda cared about me. To me, that counted more than reputation or equipment.

We were fighting an uphill battle, and we had no control over it. It was time to move forward and get back to the chemo. I would do it at Bethesda with my family down the street and staff who cared about me. Dave also got here on this day. It was good to have him back. My support system was in place and it was time to get to it. So they plugged the bag of chemo in and started round two.

TUESDAY, SEPTEMBER 1, 2009

Day one of chemotherapy has started

Dear Family and Friends,

Bob's doctor started him on chemotherapy last night at 6:00 p.m. He receives it via IV and it takes a few hours to get through. He got his second bag of chemo this morning at 6:00 a.m. He is a bit nauseous but doing OK. He will get his next round at 6:00 p.m. on Wednesday night. He seems very mobile and is trying to keep his weight up. Yesterday, they weighed him and he was 198 lbs. (That is up by about 15 lbs from a few weeks ago.) Dave is here and is taking great care of him during the day.

I'd like to especially thank Traci Tate today. With running two businesses and her kids starting school, it's incredible that she can sacrifice her husband for a week to take care of Bob while I work. I am truly grateful and appreciative.

Please keep Bob in your thoughts and prayers.

Love and thanks,

— Michele

I was finally able to look in the mirror without cringing at how much weight I had lost. I had been very scrawny not too long ago. I was still dealing with my bed wound, but overall the first couple of days had gone OK. I also want to thank Traci Tate for everything she has done for me. She is a friend I can always count on.

Having Dave back was a huge help to both Michele and me. He made me eat and helped with my rehabilitation sessions. Getting me to eat was a big deal. My stomach was still trying to get used to actual food. I had really grown to like my daily milkshake. I also was eating a lot of popsicles. My throat was still sore from the breathing tube. The popsicles really helped by cooling the inflamed area.

THURSDAY, SEPTEMBER 3, 2009

Spinal tap today...not the movie either...

Dear Family and Friends,

Bob has finished his second day of chemotherapy and has one more day to go. This morning the chief of surgery came into his room and wanted to put a scope up his nose and down into his throat to see the reason why Bob hasn't been able to speak as well as he should. (He still sounds very hoarse and like Darth Vader.) Bob refused the scope, and I chased after the surgeon and asked if he could come back next week. He said he would try.

I think Bob was just a bit overloaded this morning because his oncologist told him she wanted to do a spinal tap today to see if the leukemia was in his spinal cord and brain. I've seen this procedure done on television and it looks like it hurts like hell. I'll give an update once this happens.

Bob's friend Dave, who has been staying with Bob this week, has started a "Lift Strong" line of apparel and merchandise. It just launched on his website on September 1, 2009. All proceeds from the sale of this gear go toward the Leukemia and Lymphoma Society. Bob is not the only person who has been affected by this disease in the powerlifting community. The things that can be accomplished when a group of committed individuals get together for a common goal are amazing. If you are interested in any of the merchandise or in reading about other cancer survivors affected by this disease, I encourage you to check out Dave's posts at www.elitefts.com/documents/liftstrong09.htm. To view the apparel, visit www.elitefts.com/liftstrong.

Thanks again to everyone for their prayers and words of encouragement for Bob. He really appreciates it.

Love and thanks,

— Michele

When I first went into the hospital back in June, they jammed a camera down my nose to look for the bleeding. It hurt like hell. I wasn't going to be doing that again right now. Honestly, the camera down the nose just scared me. The spinal tap scared the shit out of me too. It hurt. It wasn't as bad as a bone marrow aspiration, but it still wasn't fun.

I still hadn't seen my butt. When I laid down, I knew it was bad. The nurse for the spinal tap said, "That's the worst bed wound

I've ever seen." My butt was still killing me, and we didn't seem to be able to make any progress on getting it better. I'm sure it didn't help that my immune system was completely shot.

My illness and Alwyn's really hit Dave hard. He wanted to do something that would really help, so he created the "Lift Strong" line of clothes. If you're looking to help raise money for the Leukemia and Lymphoma Society (LLS), please visit www.elitefts.com and buy a T-shirt. All the money goes to LLS.

FRIDAY, SEPTEMBER 4, 2009

Bob possibly coming home Monday!!!

Dear Family and Friends,

I don't want to jinx it, but the doctor said that if Bob can show he isn't actively bleeding and it's safe for him, she's going to let him go home on Monday!! His counts dropped a little bit today, but that was to be expected. He's having a lot of joint pain and has his last day of chemo today. Please wish him well!

Bob's friend Dave left us today to go back to Ohio. He was such a help to me during this week, watching Bob while I worked. I can't thank him enough!

Please keep Bob in your thoughts and prayers, and I'll update his progress over the weekend. Have a fun and safe Labor Day!!

Love and thanks,

— Michele

Dave headed home, but he had made a difference in my life that I can never repay him for. Thank you, brother. The thought of going home was great and terrifying all at once. I was excited to be free of hospitals for the first time in months. I was also scared that if anything happened I would be on my own. Once again, my family bonded together to make sure I was under constant supervision.

I think I was mostly scared to be out of the hospital because I had grown used to it. In many ways, I had started to rely on the constant supervision. I was used to seeing a nurse or doctor every couple hours. I still had all these holes and wounds in me. Was it really safe for me to go home? At first, all I wanted to do was go home, but now I was afraid to leave.

MONDAY, SEPTEMBER 7, 2009

The eagle has landed...Bob is home!!!!

Dear Family and Friends,

It is with great joy that I can finally say Bob is home!! He got home late last night. I made the couch up for him today, and he is getting around with a cane in the house. Christopher stopped by to visit today for about an hour, and he and I played while Bob watched. The smile that came across Bob's face was priceless. It is a time for happiness and celebration.

Bob's counts are still low. According to the doctor, they may be dropping still, so Bob may have to go into the hospital on an outpatient basis for a blood transfusion every couple of days. Tomorrow I'm going to go back to work, and Bob is going to spend the day with his parents.

I can't even begin to thank everyone for all the love and support provided to Bob and me over the past seventy something days. Bob still has two more rounds of chemotherapy over the next two months. I will still be keeping up this blog daily as his progress continues, so please keep reading!! He still has a long road to recovery.

Love and thanks,

— Michele

It was great to get home but scary. I had planned to sleep on the couch but slept in the bed instead. If you haven't figured it out by now, I can be very pigheaded. We have a two-story house, and I proceeded to climb the stairs. As I reached the halfway point, I really questioned my decision to climb the stairs. I was out of breath, but I was committed now. So I took my time and lumbered up the rest of the way. I was exhausted by the time I got to the top.

It was great to have Christopher over. It was like Christmas and my birthday all in one. I was finally home, and he was running around. I couldn't do much but lay there. It made me feel so good to watch CT and Michele play. It was another small victory on my road to recovery.

After he left, I cried again. All I could think about was Michele and Christopher having to live without me. If you can't tell by now, my emotions were a wreck. I don't know if it was the chemo or just everything going on, but my emotional swings were very hard for me to handle. I'm sure they weren't easy for Michele to deal with either. Not only was she trying to hold herself together, but she had to try and keep me from breaking down. How would you like that responsibility?

THURSDAY, SEPTEMBER 10, 2009

Bob's platelets dropped to 8000—transfusion needed

Dear Family and Friends,

Bob has been out of the hospital for the last four days. He has been doing well at home and spending the afternoons at his parent's house. It gives him the opportunity to see Christopher and eat his mom's famous "macaroni and tuna fish," which he eats by the truckload!

He went to see the oncologist today, and they said his platelets have dropped dramatically to 8000. He is back at Bethesda now having a platelet transfusion on an outpatient basis. I am very concerned that he may become neutropenic over the next few days and will have to start wearing a mask so he doesn't get any infections. He has two wounds still that he's dealing with—the tracheotomy in his throat and the stage 3 bedsore wound. I have gotten pretty good at taking care of these wounds, but we have an appointment with a wound care center tomorrow so that I can get proper training in dressing them for him. Bob wanted me to tell everyone thank you for all the help and support he has received. I will follow up tomorrow and let you know how he's doing.

Love and thanks,

— Michele

I was doing OK now. I was still weak, but we had a routine going. I would get up, and my Dad would come pick me up. I would head over to my parents and spend the day on the couch watching television. My mom would pick up CT from school, and he would spend the afternoon with me. We would watch iCarly, Hannah Montana, *and other shows that a six year old watches. We also did homework and caught up on all the missed time from when I was really sick. Michele would stop by on her way home from work and pick me up to go home.*

I must say there is nothing like going to your parents' house to make you feel better. This isn't the home I grew up in, as my parents relocated to Florida from Connecticut in 2004, but it was still my parents' house. I had my mom making me my favorite foods and my Dad discussing the current events with me. With the war on terrorism going on, my dad was able to add some unique views. I really enjoyed just sitting around and spending time with my parents. I really needed that rehabilitation for my soul. Having CT there every afternoon just made it even better.

Once home, Michele had to play nurse to my wounds. I kept telling everyone that there was still a small hole in my throat. Everyone thought I was nuts. My butt simply wouldn't heal. With my immune system shot, my body didn't care that my butt hurt like hell. Michele wrote up a schedule of which drugs to take and when and when we needed to change bandages. She was extremely organized and really kept me on track. I'm not really a very good patient. She swallowed her frustration and got me to do the right thing when scheduled.

MONDAY, SEPTEMBER 14, 2009

Bob's blood dropping again

Dear Family and Friends,

This morning Bob went to his oncologist. Over the weekend, his platelets dropped to 8000 and his hemoglobin to 6.5. The doctor gave Bob the option of either being readmitted to the hospital or going in on an outpatient basis for transfusions today. Needless to say, he chose outpatient, and I dropped him off at Bethesda at 9:00 a.m. It's 6:00 p.m. now and he's still at it. They gave him two red blood transfusions, two platelets, and a magnesium IV. He is tired but in good spirits. The doctor said he will need chemo up until December, so it looks like we won't be having our welcome home/engagement party until January.

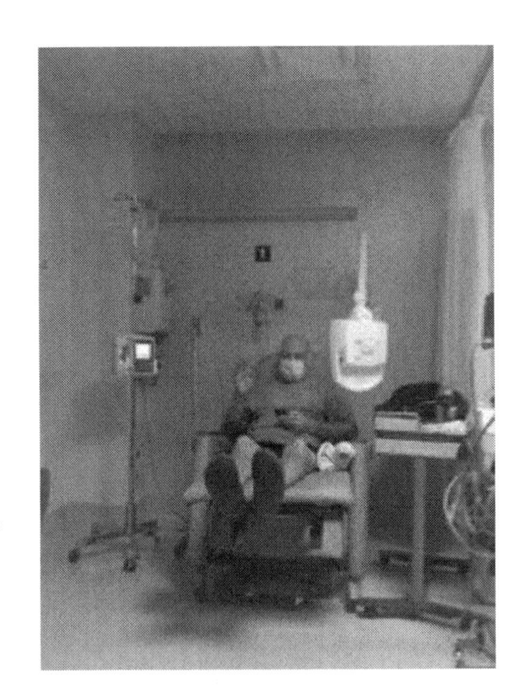

Please keep Bob in your thoughts and prayers.

Love and thanks,

— Michele

My visits to the Infusion Center became very frequent. Again, the nurses were top notch. They knew my mom from her various treatments and visits. I passed the day watching the small individual televisions that they had at the stations. It beat being in the hospital overnight, and the staff were great.

After the first visit, I figured out what I needed to pack in my backpack to get through my infusion session. I brought everything I needed and set up shop. This is where I saw how patients can be abusive. The Infusion Center is basically shaped like an "L." Each person has an individual station along the wall. Some of the patients treated the nurses like crap. Why? These girls busted their butts. People complained about everything you can imagine. It made me angry that these great nurses were being treated poorly by people who were just being asses.

TUESDAY, SEPTEMBER 15, 2009

Bob taken to emergency room

Dear Family and Friends,

When I got home from work today, I went to pick Bob up from his parents' house. When I got there, he was complaining that he was nauseous. We took his temperature and it was 101° F. I called his oncologist, and she wanted us to immediately bring him into the emergency room. She said that because he's on antibiotics, he shouldn't be getting a fever, and if he is, it can't be good. We are sitting in the emergency room right now. They've done a million blood tests, and so far, his platelets are at 20,000 (normal is between 150,000—450,000), and his white count is at 0.3. We're waiting for the rest of the tests. In the meanwhile, they gave him a chest x-ray, IV fluids, and Vancomycin. I'm very worried about Bob and will stay with him as long as it takes or until they get him stable. Please keep Bob in your thoughts and prayers tonight. He's going to need it.

Love and thanks,

— Michele

I was laying on the couch at my parents, and I knew I was sick. I could tell I had a temperature. I didn't want to admit it, but I knew I had to go back into the hospital. The worst part was that I didn't have a PICC line in at this point, so I had to repeatedly get stuck with needles. After five or six times of getting stuck, it starts to get to you. The emergency room nurse was incredible. I was in a lot of pain, and she got me medicated first and then started on all the blood draws. They had to do several special blood tests, which meant I was going to get stuck a lot. She felt so bad for me that she gave me my second injection of pain meds early. I felt like a pincushion.

Emotionally, I was scared to my core. I knew fevers could kill chemo patients. The Dr. had told me about one of her patients who let her 101° F fever go too long and it cost that patient her life. So this simple fever could be life-threatening. I tried to stay calm, but that voice in the back of my head was screaming at me.

WEDNESDAY, SEPTEMBER 16, 2009

Bob back on cancer wing, will be here awhile

Dear Family and Friends,

Last night, they admitted Bob back to the cancer wing. They gave him blood, platelets, and antibiotics throughout the night. Unfortunately, when the oncologist came to visit this morning, none of his counts had come up. He still has a fever, albeit a low-grade one. We had a consultation with the infectious disease doctor as well. He is taking cultures of Bob's tracheotomy site and bedsore site to see if they are infected and he's getting Bob an MRI to see if the bedsore wound got deep enough to infect bones in his back. In addition, they have to put a PICC line in, but his platelets are still too low. So they stuck poor Bob a million times for IVs and blood. He's nauseous, tired, and in lots of pain.

Please keep him in your thoughts and prayers.

Love and thanks,

— Michele

I continued to be a pincushion. Everyone was very worried about my butt. I was also getting sick of the pain in my butt. I spent a lot of time on my butt because I really couldn't stand for too long. According to Michele, my butt was still a mess. All the antibiotics made me more nauseous, if that was possible. I was right back to full on 'take the pain and keep fighting mode.'

The butt wound was also very embarrassing. Imagine having to roll over several times a day so doctors and nurses can look at your butt. You lose all modesty in a hospital after a while. I think it might be the gowns. Can't they come up with something better? I somehow got used to showing the world my butt.

WEDNESDAY, SEPTEMBER 16, 2009

Fourteen hours later and no blood still

Dear Family and Friends,

It's almost 11:00 p.m., and to say that today has been frustrating would be a severe understatement. Bob's oncologist came in around 8:30 a.m. and ordered blood and platelets for him. We are still waiting on them. If you have been following this blog from the beginning, you know this has been an issue before. Bethesda contracts with the Big Red Bus, which is a community blood center out of Orlando. They are waiting for blood to get here from there.

My girlfriend is the director of the rival blood bank of south Florida and has previously told me that whatever blood Bob needed they would send over in a matter of minutes, but Bethesda hospital has refused. Time and time again I have asked. It's 11:00 p.m. and still no blood. In addition, Bob has now spiked a fever of 103° F. The nurse told me she ordered him a cooling blanket. That was an hour and a half ago. I swiped some ice from the supply room, stuffed it into rubber gloves, and put them under Bob's arms to try and lower his fever. Tonight's nurse is *useless*.

Here's the icing on today's cake. They came to get Bob for an MRI. He wanted me to go with him. As the transporter wheeled Bob out of the room, another transporter wheeled a person two doors down out in a body bag to the morgue. We had to wait next to the

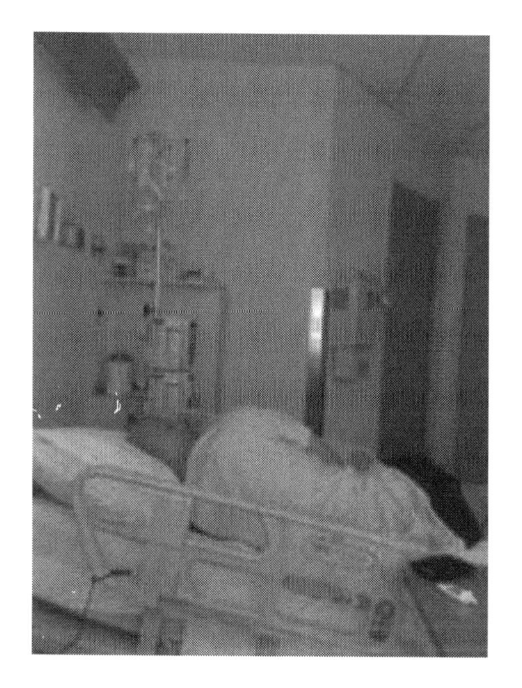

body bag while we took the elevator to the basement. I asked Bob if he was OK. He said yes, but it freaked me out.

The MRI was one of the closed ones. It's tight as a coffin without any room to breathe. As soon as they pushed Bob in, he freaked out. He couldn't do it, and I couldn't blame him after what he saw, not to mention he had a fever and was in pain and exhausted. That was our day.

The only bright spot for Bob was they gave him a pain pump that he could push every eight minutes. It gave him 1 mg of Dilaudid. He was previously getting 2 mg of Dilaudid every two hours. I'm no mathematician, but that's like 15 mg of Dilaudid every two hours if he presses it every eight minutes, which he's been doing.

When I pointed this out to the nurse, she assured me that the pain pump distributes the medication differently than an injection, but I think she's an idiot and I don't believe her. I'm exhausted and have had it up to here tonight. I'm going to raise some hell about getting Bob some proper ice packs.

Bob needs lots of prayers tonight, and I need a stiff drink...

Love and thanks,

— Michele

All I could do was worry about what I could control. So when the blood got there, it got there. There was nothing I could do about that. But we needed to get the fever under control, so it was more ice bags all over me. I didn't get any sleep at all. The anxiety of the fever was really eating at me.

Yeah, the person being wheeled out in the body bag got to me. I knew that could be me, and I also knew it was a shitty way to die. That poor person was wheeled down the hall and taken down the elevator. Somehow that person deserved better. It really shook me. It was like I was always reminded of how serious my situation was. When I got down to the MRI, there wasn't any way in hell I could get in that coffin. I had to fight back puking in the booth. Then I thought I would drown in my own puke if the woman didn't get back in the room quickly.

I hated the pain pump. Life was much better for me when they just gave me my Dilaudid every couple of hours. The problem with the pump is you need to push it every eight minutes. If you don't, the pain mounts. So I got even less sleep. I would fall asleep and wake up in terrible pain because I hadn't pushed the button. I felt like a slave to the clock, and I really didn't like it at all.

THURSDAY, SEPTEMBER 17, 2009

We got platelets 24 hours later; no blood yet

Dear Family and Friends,

After writing the blog last night, I went out and spoke to the charge nurse about getting Bob some ice packs. She was nasty to me and told me to sit in the room and wait for the nurse. I was so mad I was beside myself. I called the nursing supervisor for the entire hospital and complained. Two minutes later, my ice packs magically arrived. Ten minutes after that, so did the cooling blanket. The dumb nurse set the blanket on 45° F, and after ten minutes, Bob had had enough. He said he'd rather die than freeze like that. I tried to explain that I could increase the temp to 98.6° F like they did in the ICU, but it was too late. He couldn't be convinced. I just had to take it off. He used ice the rest of the night. Although Bob had a fever throughout the night, the nurse didn't bother to give him Tylenol until 7:00 a.m.

At 6:00 a.m., I had to call down to the blood bank to give them hell and find out where the blood was. The blood had arrived, but no one seemed to be in a rush to bring it up. Bob received the platelets at 10:00 a.m., and we're now waiting on the red blood. Bob's temperature is still at 102° F. He's packed in ice, is nauseous, and refuses to eat. I talked him into one Jell-O and a Gatorade. The infectious disease doctor came in, and we told him about the MRI debacle. He said they'd do a CT instead. When Bob realized he had to drink contrast dye, he refused. That's been our day thus far.

Please keep Bob in your thoughts and prayers.

P.S. They put Bob on a morphine PCA pump, not Dilaudid, and he's getting 1 mg every eight minutes.

Love and thanks,

— Michele

To say that blanket was cold is an understatement. I was freezing and it was horribly painful. Imagine laying on a piece of ice in a hospital gown. No way was I up for that. I could handle the ice packs, but that blanket was too much. I did tell Michele that I would rather die than lay on that thing anymore. That's how bad it was.

The infectious disease doctor wanted me to do a CT scan, which was fine, but I couldn't even eat or drink regular food. How on earth was I going to drink all of that dye? Sometimes I don't think the specialists bother to read the charts.

The morphine pump proved to be my undoing. It didn't help with my pain and it seemed to be upsetting my stomach. I was in pain and felt like I was going to vomit at any moment. I was really developing a true dislike for the pain pump.

FRIDAY, SEPTEMBER 18, 2009

Infection at tracheotomy site in neck

Dear Family and Friends,

Tonight was a rough night for Bob. He spent the night nauseous and throwing up every hour (even though he didn't eat anything all day). We think it might be from switching from the Dilaudid to the morphine. The nurse had to give him Ambien just so he could get some sleep.

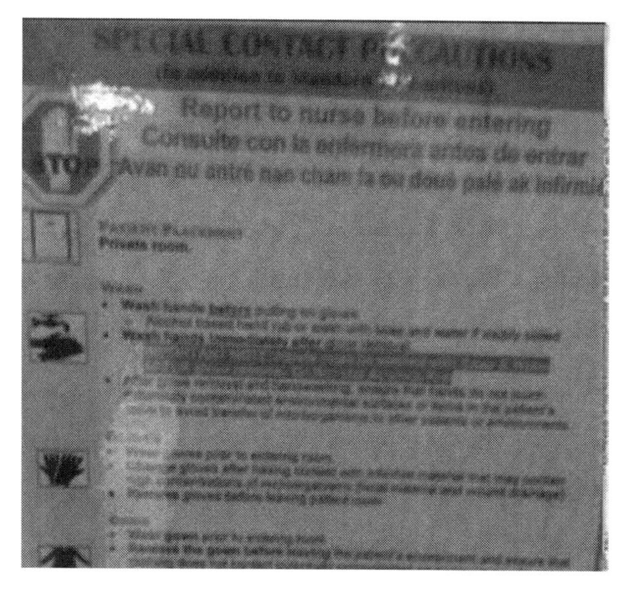

When we woke up this morning, the nurse came in and hung a precaution sign on Bob's door, which said that anyone coming in had to wear a mask, gloves, and blue gown. She said Bob has some type of infection at the wound site in his neck. It takes three days or so to figure out exactly what he has because they grow it in a Petri dish. We're still waiting.

Bob is tired, sore, and miserable. He isn't checking his email, texts, or phone calls.

Please keep Bob in your thoughts and prayers.

Love and thanks,

— Michele

This was my worst night in chemo. I puked and puked until there wasn't anything left. Then I dry heaved, and on it went. It started right as Michele was about to take a break. She was walking out of the room to go to the cafeteria and get something to eat. I sat up fast and grabbed for the puke bucket. Michele turned and headed to me to help. She was trying to help hold the bucket, and I puked all over her arms. How's that for gratitude?

I had an infection in my neck wound site and I'm sure I had one in my butt wound as well. My butt still looked like hamburger meat, and my neck was full of puss and looked like I had just been cut with a knife. My body was so consumed with fighting the cancer it didn't have time for infections, but I was still in the fight.

This was a miserable day. My body ached so badly from all the puking. My neck hurt like hell. My butt hurt like hell. Every part of my body hurt like hell. I couldn't find a position to lay in that didn't hurt. The pain pump didn't help. I was really feeling down on this day. I just wanted the day to be over.

SATURDAY, SEPTEMBER 19, 2009

Bob feeling better...

Dear Family and Friends,

I'm happy to report that Bob is feeling much better today. He doesn't have any nausea, vomiting, or fevers! Also, the doctor decided to put Bob's blood on standby (genius idea), and when he needed blood yesterday, he got it in fifteen minutes. It's funny how effective a squeaky wheel is!

Bob is much happier being back on Dilaudid rather than morphine. The doctor also said that Bob has MRSA in his neck and backside. They had him on Vancomycin but had to change it because he developed hearing issues.

Bob's appetite is back, so I know he's getting better, and he's checking his emails too.

Lots of love and thanks,

— Michele

The Dr. put me back on injectable Dilaudid, and I was a happy camper again. Most people prefer the pain pump, but the injections worked much better for me. The Vancomycin caused me to lose my hearing. It has that effect on some people. With everything else I had going on, I couldn't deal with losing my hearing. I could barely talk, and I had infections all over the place. How much can one man handle?

I kept up with my support network through emails and texts. It helped to keep me busy and keep my mind off all the medical junk. Having a hand-held device was really big for me. It allowed me to keep in touch with everyone without hobbling over to the laptop and sitting in the hard chair.

When you are in chemotherapy, your world is very small. I had the television and that was about it. The chemo also wreaked havoc on my eyesight. It does that with most people. I had some magazines and books, but the words were a blur. I am usually a big reader, but I just couldn't see the words. Again, I was left with too much time to think. The battle between being positive and negative was constant.

SUNDAY, SEPTEMBER 20, 2009

Bob might be going home Monday!

Dear Family and Friends,

After a couple days without a fever and increasing white cell counts (thanks to Neupogen injections), the oncologist said that as long as Bob is willing to go home with a PICC line and get IV antibiotics every day for the MRSA, they might let him go home tomorrow. Needless to say, he was very happy to hear the news. Christopher stopped by to see him, which made him happy too. Although Bob is tired, he is in good spirits. Please continue to keep him in your prayers and thoughts.

Love and thanks,

— Michele

Things started heading back in the right direction. I had a bunch of little victories today. My counts were improving and that was a big deal for me to hear. It made me feel like the chemo was working. Getting to go home was also a great goal to have dangled in front of me. I would much rather be parked on my couch than in a hospital bed. CT's visits always gave me strength. I got to see my reason for living right in front of me. I wasn't going to let him grow up without a father.

TUESDAY, SEPTEMBER 22, 2009

Bob coming home today

Dear Family and Friends,

They kept Bob an extra day yesterday because they wanted to load him up with blood, magnesium, and potassium IVs so he wouldn't have to get any more this week. They are saving his IV lines for the antibiotics for the MRSA. I changed the dressing on his tracheotomy site last night and it's still infected. I'm hoping once he gets home it will get better.

As most of you know, I bought Bob a Blackberry so he could keep up with his emails while he was in the hospital. He didn't like the internet connection (so he said...I think he was jealous that both Dave and I have iPhones), and now he wants an iPhone. So I bought him an iPhone today. He won't get it until I get off work, but I think he's going to be happy with it.

Please keep Bob in your thoughts and prayers. He goes back into the hospital on September 31, 2009 for the second round of consolidation chemotherapy.

Love and thanks,

— Michele

The Dr. talked me into the extra day with little resistance on my part. Loading me up on blood seemed like the smart thing to do. Michele had to become part nurse in addition to everything else she was juggling. She did great and kept the dressings changed and cleaned. I still kept telling everyone that there was a hole in my trach wound site. Still, no one believed me, but I could feel it.

The iPhone became my savior. Now that I was much more mentally with it, I needed something to occupy me. The iPhone allowed me to keep up with all my emails and texts. It also gave me access to the internet. When I went back in for future chemo treatments, I lived on my iPhone. I could actually read it because I could make the text size larger. I'm not sure what I would have done without it.

SUNDAY, SEPTEMBER 27, 2009

Bob heading back for round three of five

Dear Family and Friends,

Bob is doing pretty well. He was happy to see his friends, Mike and Ed, yesterday who came from New York City and Ft. Meyers, respectively, to see him. We had lunch and Bob got to do some catching up. This morning we went back to the hospital for antibiotic infusions and then over to my parents for lunch.

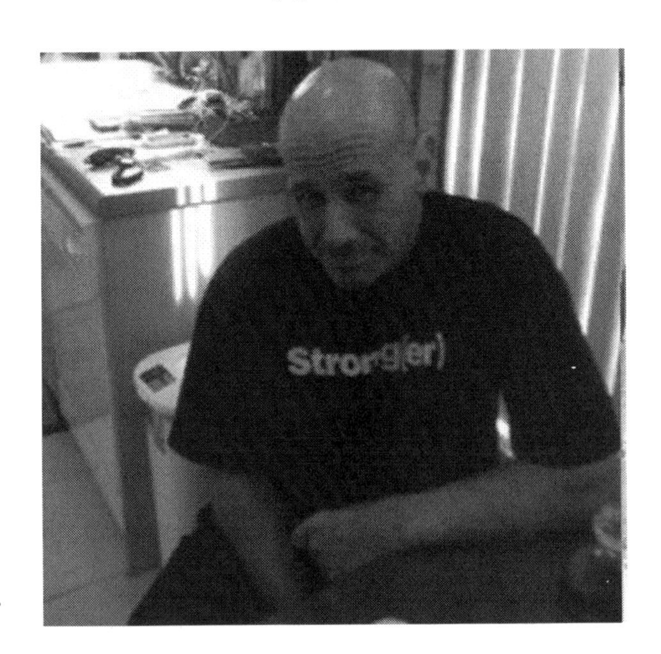

Now we are hanging out with Christopher and hanging Halloween decorations.

Please keep Bob in your thoughts and prayers as he heads back into the hospital.

P.S. Bob wanted me to say hi to everyone for him.

Love and thanks,

— Michele

Mike Stuchiner and Ed Rectenwald came to visit. It felt great to see them. We sat around and stuffed our faces and reminisced. For a couple hours, life was normal again. I was starting to get mentally ready to head back into the hospital. I was also starting to get all my hospital gear in order. After being in hospitals for so long, I had figured out what I needed to bring when I went in. I also had my room set up exactly as I wanted before they started the chemo. I guess you could say I had developed my chemo routine, and I was ready for round three. How bad is that—a chemo routine? The fight went on, and I wasn't about to stop fighting. I had too much to live for.

TUESDAY, SEPTEMBER 29, 2009

Day one of round three chemotherapy complete

Dear Family and Friends,

Day one of Bob's chemotherapy is finished, and I must say Bob is in good spirits. Before chemotherapy started, his counts were higher than they had ever been—335,000 for platelets and 11 for hemoglobin. His white count was in the normal range as well. Bob hasn't had any fevers in the past week, but he has suffered from a screwed up internal temperature system. He has the thermostat set at 65° F, and he's sweating through all his clothing. The doctor said it could be a side effect from the chemo, but as long as he doesn't have a temperature, everything is OK. They tested him again last night for MRSA in his neck area. I'm assuming it's going to come back positive again. Other than that, Bob's in good spirits. The doctor said that as long as things go well, they can get him out of the hospital as early as Saturday, which would be great!

Please continue to keep Bob in your thoughts and prayers.

Love and thanks,

— Michele

I now had a good understanding of how the week would go. Day one and day two would go OK, but the real pain would start on day three. I knew it was coming, and I knew my job was to take it. For this round, I had a new development—sweating. I mean like a river. I couldn't keep my gowns or bed dry. I went though towels by the cartload. The chemo does many things and sweating was one of them. The sweats plagued me for the rest of my chemo sessions. I didn't have a temperature, but I would just break out in downpours of sweat without any warning. It was just one more thing that kept me from sleeping.

FRIDAY, OCTOBER 2, 2009

Chemo a success so far; Bob coming home tomorrow...

Dear Family and Friends,

Bob is holding his own very well with regards to the chemotherapy. His blood counts are holding steady and so are his platelets. The doctor said Bob will be going home tomorrow. Bob is looking forward to eating real food (as opposed to hospital food) and getting to have Christopher come over to our house to play video games. The only issue I'm dealing with now is Bob's insurance company. I'm fighting with them to get Bob long-term disability. They are making us prove that Bob's leukemia isn't a pre-existing condition (which is ridiculous).

Please keep Bob in your thoughts and prayers. As soon as he gets out tomorrow, I'll take a picture of him and post it so you can see his progress. He's been mainly living off Snickers bars and Whatchamacalits because the hospital food isn't the greatest, so he's putting on a few pounds.

Love and thanks,

— Michele

Michele had to deal with all kinds of insurance issues. She had issues with both health and disability insurance. I'll just say that these companies don't make things easy when you really need them. Michele had to fight to get me the insurance I had paid for, but she came through as always. Her strength was amazing. What a fighter she is in her own right.

For some reason, the hospital food was really unappealing to me this week. I ate a lot of candy bars and Burger King. Alwyn yelled at me because carbs are what cancer cells thrive on, so I had to change things around in my diet. Chemo seems to also make everything taste metallic. Nothing really tasted good to me. Some things were better than others, but nothing really tasted good anymore. I lived on my mom's macaroni and tuna fish. You know how you have that special dish only mom can make? Well for me, it was my mom's macaroni and tuna fish. I ate it four times a day. I also became addicted to Jell-O and Italian Ice. They both made my sore throat feel better. My family made sure I always had a constant supply of both in refrigerator in my room.

TUESDAY, OCTOBER 6, 2009

Bob is home and happy

Dear Family and Friends,

Sorry it's been a few days since I've updated the blog. Bob is home now and doing pretty well. He's been trying to sleep as much as possible. I'm going with him to the doctor tomorrow so they can show me how to flush his PICC line. His counts are doing surprising well so far too.

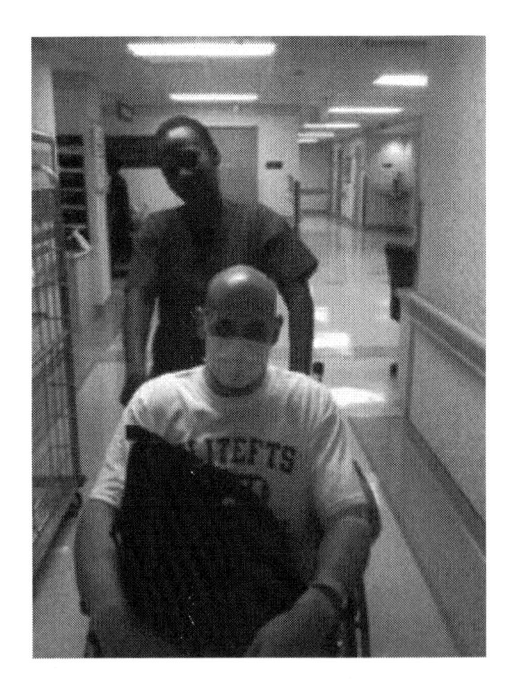

Please continue to keep Bob in your thoughts and prayers.

Love and thanks,

— Michele

Life now started to have a routine—one week of chemo and three weeks at home recovering. Michele continued in her nursing role and added skills as needed. My trach hole and butt wound continued to be issues. I pretty much spent my days laying on the couch sleeping and watching television with Michele at night. Things seemed to be moving along smoothly considering how chaotic the past four months had been. Life was really starting to settle into a routine.

We tried all kinds of different combinations of ointments and bandages on my butt and throat. No matter what we tried, we couldn't seem to make progress. When I was in the hospital, I was very lucky to have a great wound care nurse. She knew my mom well and kept working on a combination that would fix me. She tried every trick she had in her book.

But I was really getting frustrated with both wounds. This issue had been going on for months, and we really hadn't made much progress. The neck wound was OK. It was a huge inconvenience to be unable to speak, but I could handle the wound. The butt wound was a nightmare. I really couldn't stand for too long, so I was constantly either sitting or laying down. My butt didn't get much chance to heal, but it was also causing constant pain. Now I know what a pain in the butt really is.

SATURDAY, OCTOBER 10, 2009

Bob hanging in there...

Dear Family and Friends,

Bob is hanging in there. He's been napping a lot. Unfortunately, his blood counts have been dropping steadily. His platelets were at 6000. Normal is 150,000–350,000. He went in as an outpatient yesterday for two units of platelets. He's keeping busy today watching football and wanted to say hi to everyone.

Please continue to keep him in your thoughts and prayers.

P.S. Thanks to Powerhouse Gym for the T-shirt and 'Get Well' card. That was so thoughtful!

Love and thanks,

— Michele

Heading into the Infusion Center at Bethesda a couple times per week became part of my routine. As I said before, the nurses were great. They did their best to get

me in and out as quickly as possible. I kept trying to look at what I could and couldn't control. I couldn't control my blood counts, so I just rolled with it. What else could I do?

TUESDAY, OCTOBER 20, 2009

Bob doing well; going back in for next round on Monday...

Dear Family and Friends,

Sorry it's been ten days since my last post. Things here have been hectic but good. The good news first—Bob has been doing fantastic on his blood counts His white blood and platelets are back in the normal ranges, and his hemoglobin is at 9.6, which is pretty high for him. Bob has been very tired and spends most days sleeping on the couch. We are working with his doctor on tweaking his pain medication, which causes him to twitch, especially at night when he gets tired. They are trying to wean him off the pain patches first. Bob is still having issues with his tracheotomy site. At one point, it looked like it was getting better. Then we decided it would be a good idea to put Neosporin on it and now it's getting worse. While Bob is in the hospital next Monday for his next round of chemo, they are going to have the surgeon look at it. I don't know how well that will go seeing as Bob won't let them look up his nose to get to his throat, but we'll see.

I'm still fighting for Bob to get long-term disability. They have approved it finally after a month but won't disperse it until I get a letter from one of his doctors from 2008 stating that he was receiving muscle relaxers for his back pain, not for cancer. It's just ridiculous. In addition, I received a phone call last week from Bob's work advising me that Bob had been laid off. Thank God my company offers domestic partner medical and dental benefits, or Bob would be screwed. Cobra wanted almost $600 a month for medical alone. In addition, Bob has racked up over $1,000,000 in medical costs (yep, that's a Million with a capital 'M!'). It's pretty screwed up. The insurance company tells you that you have a $5000 co-pay, but then once you've reached that, they tell you they'll only pay 90 percent. So Bob's portion of the medical bills for the last four months is $100,000 out of pocket. Nice. I think we're better off living in Canada or Switzerland or something, but Bob won't have any of that. Sorry for the complaining, but it gets very frustrating fighting with these companies. At least Bob has Aetna now. I'm hoping they are much better.

Please continue to keep Bob in your thoughts and prayers. He'll be in the hospital Monday, October 26 and will get out on Halloween afternoon—just in time to watch Christopher trick or treat!!

P.S. I'll make sure to post some pictures of Bob soon.

Love and thanks,

— Michele

The pain patches made me twitch violently. When they took me off them, the twitches went away, so I wasn't a big fan of the pain patches. The issues continued with my trach site and butt wound and rolled on without any end in sight. Again, I kept telling everyone that I still had a hole in my trach site. No one believed me. Yeah, I was getting frustrated.

The company I worked for laid me off in the middle of everything else I had going on. The insurance issues continued for Michele and she kept on fighting them. The medical bills were piling up by the thousands. I pretty much ignored all of it. What could they do to me? Kill me? You see cancer puts things in perspective. I was consumed with trying to live, and everything else would have to wait.

Don't get me wrong—in the back of my mind, the bills were a burden. I knew my credit would be shot. But what could I do? I think I owe over $300,000. I simply don't have that kind of money laying around. I've also always worked in the mortgage industry, and my credit can affect whether or not I get a job. I'm hoping I can explain the situation to any future, potential employers and they'll be sympathetic.

MONDAY, OCTOBER 26, 2009

Bob back in hospital...

Dear Family and Friends,

Bob is back in the hospital for his second to last round of chemotherapy. He's in good spirits (as you can see from the photo) but still very tired all the time.

He's going into this round with high counts, which is good, but he's still having issues with the tracheotomy site. It still isn't healing. I actually think it's infected again, but Bob is stubborn and doesn't want the ear, nose, and throat doctor to look at it with a scope unless they knock him out. The doctor won't do that because of the chemo, so everyone is stuck looking at the wound from the outside only.

I'm just hoping there isn't any permanent damage to his vocal chords. He's still speaking at a whisper, and no one can understand him on the phone. That's about it. I'll be hopefully giving regular updates this week because he'll be in there until Saturday.

Please keep Bob in your thoughts and prayers.

Love and thanks,

— Michele

Time for round four. Again, I prepared and had all my ducks in a row. I got my room set up, and I was ready to roll. I had my iPhone to keep me busy. The trach was becoming a big issue because I still had no voice. We were all starting to worry that I might never be able to speak again except in a whisper. No one wanted to hear what I had to say about there still being a hole in my throat.

My biggest concern about my voice was how would I get a job? No one would hire someone who couldn't talk. Cancer had already really screwed up my life. Would I be stuck on disability for the rest of my life now too? That wasn't how I wanted to live. I became angry again at the whole thing. My life had been turned upside down and it seemed to just keep coming. I was glad my treatment really seemed to be headed in the right direction, but what about after I got better? What kind of future would I have, if any?

TUESDAY, OCTOBER 27, 2009

Bob saw the ENT doctor; going to have surgery...

Dear Family and Friends,

Thanks so much for all the encouraging words to me and Bob regarding his neck and speech. I really think it did the trick because when I woke up this morning, I got a text from Bob. He said that the ear, nose, and throat (ENT) doctor had stopped by and he had let him put the scope partially down his throat. I was very proud of him. Now for the not so good news. There is still a hole where Bob's tracheotomy site is and the doctor wants to close it. It involves placing a flap of muscle over the hole in the trachea and sewing the skin together above that. Bob wouldn't be fully knocked out but in twilight. The doctor would then put the scope down Bob's nose and see what else is wrong. The doctor said Bob's left vocal cord isn't fully functioning. The ENT doctor is going to consult with Bob's oncologist to see about a timeline for surgery, but it sounded like he wanted to do it on Halloween morning (Saturday).

I spoke with Bob's doctor last night. She said that if he had surgery, she'd prefer to do it as soon as possible because of the chemotherapy and because Bob's blood counts go down exponentially day by day as well as his immune system and ability to clot. Because I had to go to work today, I told Bob to tell the oncologist that he wants to see if they can do the surgery tomorrow. Bob's response was, "The doctors know best." I started laughing!

So needless to say, *I'm* going to call the oncologist today and see what we can do about pushing this surgery up. It doesn't make any sense to do it on Saturday—the day he's supposed to be discharged. If they did it today, at least they could observe him for a few days. One would think that would be the most logical thing, but as I have learned over the past few months, the doctor's decisions don't seem to have any rhyme or reason.

I am still fighting with Bob's insurance company trying to get him long-term disability. They won't release any checks yet. However, I did get him unemployment. Did you know the maximum unemployment rate in the state of Florida is $275 a week? What the heck can you buy for that? It's ridiculous. I've got to get this crap straightened out as soon as possible.

Please continue to keep Bob in your thoughts and prayers.

Love and thanks,

— Michele

So the ENT confirmed what I had been saying for months now. I wanted to jump up and scream, "I was right!" The only problem was I still didn't have a voice. I was really hopeful that closing this hole would be the cure my voice desperately needed. I really felt like I had gained another major victory in my healing. I had hope for my voice, and I just knew I was right.

I really started to think I was beginning to hold my own in the fight. I hadn't won yet, but I was finally holding my own. I felt like the momentum was swinging in my direction. If we could continue to keep the momentum going, I could win the fight. I didn't want to look too far down the road, but I was hoping I could eventually put the pieces of my life back together and have the life I had hoped for.

WEDNESDAY, OCTOBER 28, 2009

Surgery scheduled for Friday...

Dear Family and Friends,

After calling the oncologist and explaining how it doesn't make sense for Bob to have surgery scheduled for the same day he's supposed to be discharged (Saturday), she spoke with the ENT and they have scheduled surgery for Friday—time to be determined. I guess we'll take it and hope Bob recovers quickly before he's discharged. I also submitted the final paperwork for Bob's long-term disability claim. That was a nightmare. I'm hoping they'll finally approve him and send him the last month's worth of checks. Other than that, everything is going pretty well with Bob. He is very tired but spends his day watching *NCIS* and *CSI Miami* and playing on his iPhone. He wanted me to say hello to everyone for him.

Thanks to all who keep reading this blog. Please continue to keep Bob in your thoughts and prayers.

Love and thanks,

— Michele

I was glad Michele got the surgery moved up. I wanted to get out of the hospital as soon as possible. The week was pretty much the same, as had been the past two rounds of chemo. The end of the week was the hardest, and I was really tired all the time. It was still all about me taking the pain and moving forward. The end was in site, and I was just trying to focus on the finish line. Everything else was a blur to me. I just wanted to be done with chemo.

FRIDAY, OCTOBER 30, 2009

Bob's surgery was a success

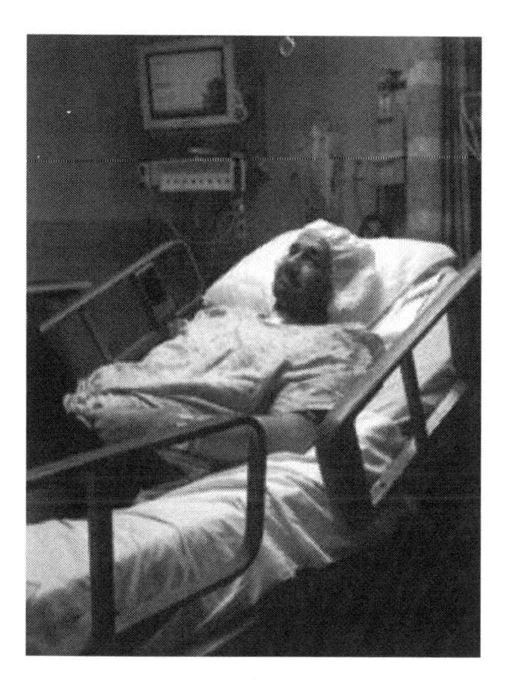

Dear Family and Friends,

Bob's surgeon just came out to see me and said everything went well. The hole in his trachea was covered by muscle, and he has five stitches that will need to be removed next week. The surgeon also looked at Bob's vocal cord and said the left one is "bowed out." At this time, there is nothing they can do about it but wait until the stitches heal. Overall, the surgery was a success. Bob is in recovery, and I'm hoping his voice is better. Thanks to everyone for your support.

Please keep Bob in your thoughts and prayers. If recovery goes well, he'll be out of here by noon tomorrow—just in time to see Christopher dressed up for Halloween.

Love and thanks,

— Michele

The surgery went well. I was groggy and sore when I woke up. The doctor talked to me, but I don't remember what he said. Michele had to tell me later that everything had gone well. I started to focus on getting ready to head home. Halloween was coming and I had to be somewhere.

I was really hoping my voice would be fixed, not right away but in time. I needed to be able to speak again. I was pretty sure I would live through this. I was really starting to think about life after chemo. How would I get back on my feet?

MONDAY, NOVEMBER 2, 2009

Bob out of hospital; doing well after surgery

Dear Family and Friends,

I hope everyone had a happy Halloween. As I said in my last post, Bob's surgery went well. That Friday I really noticed a difference in Bob's voice. He was speaking much deeper and he wasn't whispering at all. But then Saturday (most likely due to the fact that the swelling went down), Bob was back to speaking in a hoarse whisper. He is going back to the ENT surgeon Thursday or Friday this week to have the stitches removed. Once it's healed, they will begin vocal testing to see the extent of the damage to his vocal cords. I'm hoping things will get better with time.

As expected, Bob got out of the hospital on Saturday afternoon. He was in good spirits and insisted he walk out of the hospital rather than get wheeled out. (He was very stubborn about this.) In addition, he also insisted I get him a costume for Halloween so that he could trick or treat with Christopher, Uncle Tom, and me. I went out and bought us matching pirate costumes, and Bob was a real trooper. He walked his butt off. Let me tell you—it was hot as heck. Like 85° F. So hot we had to bring poor Christopher home to change out of his polyester costume and into a Red Sox T-shirt and shorts. We all had a fantastic time on Halloween. I will post photos later.

Bob and I went to his oncologist this morning so he could get a check up and a Neupogen shot. His counts are actually pretty good today, and he didn't need any blood. He'll be going back every day this week for more shots and a follow up. I also got a call from the Leukemia and Lymphoma Society of Palm Beach. They want me to participate in their Woman of the Year campaign. I have to call them back today. Bob's doctor was the one who nominated me. I was very honored that she had thought of me.

I will keep everyone posted on Bob's progress throughout the week. Please continue to keep him in your thoughts and prayers.

Love and thanks,

— Michele

Little victories add up. You'd better believe I was walking out of the hospital! There wasn't any chance of me getting in that wheelchair when they brought it in the room. I was exhausted when we got to the car. That was the furthest I had walked in almost five months, but I walked out with my head held high and my pride soaring. Another victory for me in the fight.

King Kong and his big brother couldn't have kept me from going trick or treating. That little boy had been through so much and had been so brave for his father. It was my turn to be brave and suck it up for him. I walked more than I thought I could. The smile on CT's face became my source of strength once again. I think we all needed that night. It was great that Uncle Tom was there as well. It was the best Halloween I have ever or will ever have. How could we ever top that one?

The Neupogen shots were part of my daily routine the week after chemo. They hurt like hell, but I just had to take the pain. The end was in sight now. I was starting to get some strength back, and I was really feeling like I would win. I still had the occasional doubt in the back of my mind, but for the most part, I was pretty confident.

It was a very proud moment for me when Michele was nominated for "Woman of the Year." She had done such an incredible job as my patient advocate. She deserved to be recognized for her efforts to fight for me. I look forward to leading the standing ovation when she wins. She has worked so hard on this campaign. She plans to raise well over $15,000 for LLS.

FRIDAY, NOVEMBER 6, 2009

Surgery stitches removed, throat update...

Dear Family and Friends,

Bob went by himself to the ENT surgeon this morning. He said the doctor told him the wound was healing perfectly, and his voice seems to be making progress. The stitches were removed. Time will tell if he needs further surgery or if his vocal cord will repair itself. After that, he went to the oncologist.

Bob has been getting Neupogen shots to bring up his white blood cell count this week, which is very low, as are his hemoglobin and platelets. I was very disappointed that his oncologist wasn't more proactive. I don't understand why she didn't just give him two units of red blood cells and one unit of platelets. He's going to her office on Monday morning and will probably need three units of blood and two units of platelets. Without being typed or crossed at the hospital, he'll be at Bethesda *all day* and most likely all day Tuesday. I just don't get why doctors are reactive, not proactive. I'm in no way a doctor, but I can see the trend in Bob's blood work. How could you let anyone walk around with 50 percent of the blood needed in the body and not be proactive? It is beyond me. What if something happens to Bob over the weekend? I'm just saying...it's annoying.

So it looks like Bob doesn't qualify for unemployment benefits because he is unable to look for a job. From what the lady said,

Bob couldn't work at his last job so he technically wasn't laid off due to a lack of available work. Whatever. It's ridiculous. I'm just glad I got the long-term disability straightened out. I recommend anyone getting this insurance if it's available.

Please keep Bob in your thoughts and prayers. He only has *one more round of chemotherapy left* (Thanksgiving week)!!

Lots of love and thanks,

— Michele

The ENT took out my stitches, and my voice was improving. I felt like I had been right all along about the hole in my neck. Michele got worked up about the blood. It didn't bother me. I had faith in the Dr. We also need to remember that blood is a finite commodity. We can't afford to waste it, so waiting made sense to me. That blood may have saved someone else's life.

MONDAY, NOVEMBER 9, 2009

Emergency admittance to the hospital...

Dear Family and Friends,

I'm beyond pissed off right now. I'm to the point of spitting nails. If you've been following this blog, you know that last week I ranted about the fact that no one—except for me apparently—felt Bob's blood counts were important. On Friday, Bob went to the doctor (and at that point, he should have received two units of blood). Well, no one tested his blood counts on Friday because the doctor was moving her office. I was pissed. Fast forward to yesterday...Bob's face was broken out with petechiae (looks like measles). By this morning, it had spread all over his body, and when he woke up, his tongue was twice its normal size and filled with bloody pustules. Needless to say, we rushed to the doctor. She said his low platelets were causing all of this and that he needed an emergency platelet transfusion. At this point, it took everything I had not to start yelling because this whole damn thing could have been avoided if someone would have been proactive.

So now here we sit, Bob and me at the hospital. It took an hour to get the blood results. His hemoglobin has dropped to 5.8. It's surprising to them that he is still conscious. Normal is 12–16. His platelets are at 2. Seriously. They are supposed to be at 150,000–350,000. His white cells are nonexistent, which means he doesn't have an immune system. I hope everyone can understand how frustrating this is because it all could have been prevented with some proactivity. So they are doing an emergency admittance into the hospital for Bob. I'll be here all day if you need me.

Please keep Bob in your thoughts and prayers.

Love and thanks,

— Michele

Yeah, Michele was pissed off. I was just freaked out by my tongue. Holy crap was it huge! I think the shock of the size of my tongue kept me from worrying about how sick I was. I had the little dots everywhere. I was a little freaked out, but trying to calm Michele down took up most of my energy. At this point, I still didn't have any energy. So I was back in the hospital and fighting again. I was used to it by now.

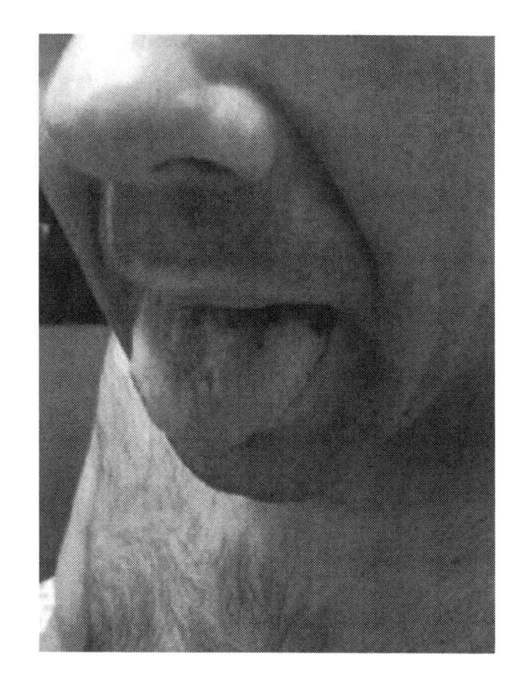

With everything we had been through, I knew we could overcome this. It was just one more bump in the road. The fight

continued, but my confidence was growing. I continued to take everything leukemia and cancer could throw at me. Now wasn't the time to worry about what could have been done differently. It was still time to fight and fight to win.

TUESDAY, NOVEMBER 10, 2009

Bob still in hospital...needs more blood still

Dear Family and Friends,

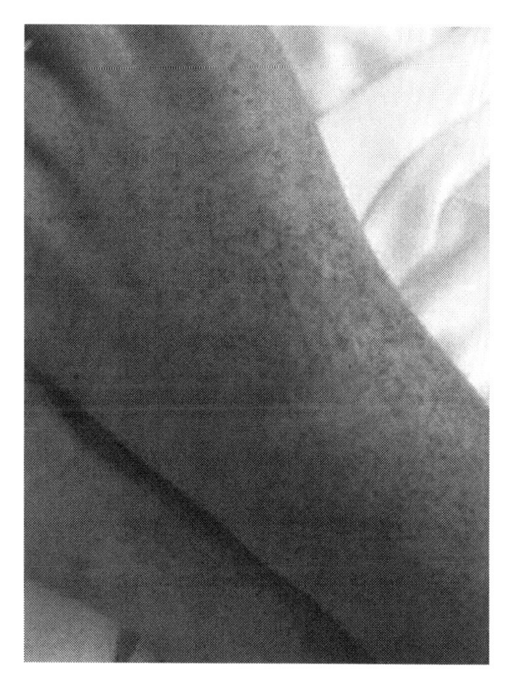

Bob is still in the hospital. He received two units of platelets and two units of packed red blood cells yesterday. He also received an additional unit of blood this morning.

Unfortunately, his counts are still low. His hemoglobin is at 7.2, and his platelets are at 26,000, so he will remain in the hospital today and receive two more units of blood. Then they will reassess.

The photo above is of Bob's foot to give you an idea of what petechiae looks like. This is what happens when you have low platelets.

The petechiae itself isn't life-threatening. If all goes well, we hope Bob will be released from the hospital early tomorrow morning. Please continue to keep him in your thoughts and prayers.

Love and thanks,

— Michele

Basically, they were pumping platelets and blood into me as fast as they could. I saw this as just another bump in the road. I was used to being in the hospital, and I was used to rolling with the punches. My only complaint was I didn't have my room set up as I would have liked because we had to rush into the hospital. I'm an anal retentive guy. Even my bed tray had to be organized a certain way. I had the hospital stay down to a science. Organization is the key. If you have to be in the hospital, make sure you have things set up. This allows you to focus on getting better. I think I drove Michele nuts with my insistence for organization. Let's just say she isn't nearly as organized as I am and that can be annoying for her. I need to have things just so. But she was a trooper and rolled with my anal retentive organization.

WEDNESDAY, NOVEMBER 11, 2009

Veteran's Day and Bob out of hospital...

Dear Family and Friends,

Bob was released from the hospital around 9:30 p.m. last night. His hemoglobin was 8.5, and his platelets were at 25,000. These are still pretty low, but he will go back to the oncologist Thursday and will more than likely need additional transfusions. Both Christopher and I have the day off today so we're going to bake cupcakes with grandma and possibly go in the pool and have a cookout with Bob's Aunt April and Uncle Tom if the weather holds up. Please continue to keep Bob in your thoughts and prayers and have a great Veteran's Day.

Love and thanks,

— Michele

Veteran's Day is a big deal to me. It's a day to honor those who give us our freedom. We usually go with my mom and dad to the UDT/SEAL Museum in Ft. Pierce, Florida. They put on a big show with real SEALs, and I love going. They do a lot of simulated SEAL stuff with helicopters and the whole nine yards. It is completely awesome to watch these professionals at work. My dad gets a chance to catch up with some old friends, and we all have a good time.

Instead, we made some cupcakes at our house. CT wanted to go in the pool, so Michele and Uncle Tom joined him. I watched for a while but got tired. Christopher had learned to swim while I was sick. He had become a pretty good swimmer and he had a great time. It made me sad that I couldn't jump in the pool with him and swim. It would have to wait, but we would make up for that later.

THURSDAY, NOVEMBER 12, 2009

Bob has a cold...and blog reflections

Dear Family and Friends,

Bob got out of the hospital late Tuesday, but yesterday he started showing signs of a cold. I was very worried last night because Bob's immune system is so weakened that any little thing can progress very quickly into something large and life-threatening. So we went to the doctor this morning. His oncologist prescribed him a Z-Pak and either Sudafed or Mucinex and said that as long as he doesn't get a fever, he should be OK. The good thing is that Bob's levels are starting to slowly go up on their own. His hemoglobin this morning was 9.9, and his platelets are at 29,000, so he won't need any transfusions today. We just have to monitor him closely for any signs of a fever, but so far he hasn't had any.

That being said, I'd like to stop for a minute and say something about this blog. I write this blog for all our family and friends to keep everyone up to date regarding Bob's progress. I know at times I can be a little harsh about what's going on, but because I have an iPhone, I have the ability to write from anywhere and usually right as everything is happening. So most of my posts are uncensored and mostly stream of consciousness. I usually don't take time to sit down and reflect before writing them. I know at times I can be hard on both the doctors and the nurses who are providing care for Bob, but I feel it's my obligation to be thorough because Bob's life is at stake. That being said, I would like to say that for the most part, I have been very impressed with the care Bob has received at Bethesda as well as with his oncologist. She is a good doctor, and I wouldn't hesitate to recommend her to anyone. I realize everyone is human and sometimes things just slip through the cracks, but I'm confident she has Bob's best interests in mind. She has gone out of her way to be there for both Bob and me throughout this process. She has been patient and has answered all of our questions. I realize that sometimes I should stop and say a few good things in this blog, so going forward, I will do more of that.

Finally, I met with the people from the Leukemia and Lymphoma Society yesterday morning regarding the "Woman of the Year" fundraising event next April, which Bob's doctor recommended me for. I have decided I will participate and try to give back to a cause that has deeply affected Bob's family. I will post more about this at a later date.

Thanks for all the recent emails and phone calls about Bob. I read all the comments posted on this blog, and even though I may not respond to all of them, they are all very much appreciated. Please continue to keep Bob in your thoughts and prayers.

Love and thanks,

— Michele

I was under the weather, but I was home. It's scary that even a cold can be life-threatening. Can you imagine the common cold killing you? I just took my medicine as the Dr. prescribed and rested. There wasn't anything else I could do. I did what I was told. I had complete faith in the Dr., and the only problem was that I still had nothing but time on my hands. Those negative thoughts had to be constantly pushed out of my head.

This was Michele's way of saying the medical people deserved some slack. It was difficult for Michele as her fiancée laid there sick. There wasn't anything she could do. So she did and still does her best to make sure I get the best possible treatment. She's great at it and I'm alive because of it. I'm sure she was frustrated because so much was out of her control.

MONDAY, NOVEMBER 16, 2009

Bob has kicked the cold and is in good spirits...

Dear Family and Friends,

Thankfully Bob has kicked his cold with minimal issues. The Z-Pak worked! In addition, he's been in good spirits, and we spent some time with Christopher over the weekend. He and Bob played *Star Wars*, and Bob's voice is coming back. His voice has improved by leaps and bounds, and he's letting his hair grow out. I swear I think he gained hair during the chemotherapy!! He has sideburns that are hilarious. I'll try to post a photo later.

Bob goes back into the hospital for his final round of chemotherapy on Monday, November 23 (during the week of Thanksgiving) and then he's done. He is very anxious to get it all over with, and I can't blame him.

Thanks for keeping him in your thoughts and prayers.

Love and thanks,

— Michele

Life was good. CT and I got to play Star Wars *on the Wii. I was starting to get my voice back, and people could actually understand me. When you go through chemo, you have too much time on your hands, so you try to find ways to occupy that time. I normally have a shaved head and shaved face. During chemo, I grew my hair out...well what was left of it. I grew some awesome 1970s side burns. I had a goatee and then a full beard. I looked different every time I went back in for chemo. The nurses wanted to know what I was going to do the next time. It helped pass the time. One more round to go, baby.*

Most of the negative thoughts had left my head. I wasn't afraid as often. I had even stopped crying for the most part. My emotions were much more in balance. I was returning to a more even-keeled mindset. I didn't think about dying any more. I really thought I was going to make it.

MONDAY, NOVEMBER 23, 2009

Bob is back at EliteFTS.com and answering questions...

Dear Family and Friends,

Bob made his first public appearance yesterday at my niece's 1st birthday party. His white blood cell counts were high enough that he could fight off any infections from 25 germy two to five year olds. Everyone was thrilled to see him and many people didn't recognize him with hair and long sideburns. (The picture I'm posting doesn't do him justice.)

Bob is back in the hospital this morning for his last round of chemotherapy. He was very anxious to get there just to be over and done with it all. (I can't blame him.) Six months of this fiasco and I'd be anxious to get it over too!

Anyway, as most of you know, Bob is very active in the powerlifting community, and for the last ten years or so, has been a fixture on the Q & A and logs at www.elitefts.com. Bob is finally strong enough to reintroduce his log.

Here's a brief excerpt:

> *"Hi everyone! For those who don't know, I was diagnosed with leukemia in June of this year. I have been undergoing chemotherapy for the past five months. During that time, there have been some complications. I was read my last rites and my family was told twice that I wouldn't make it through the night. My fiancée, Michele, has been keeping a blog from the start of this. It can be found at http://bobyoungs.blogspot.com/.*
>
> *The reason I'm doing a log now is in an effort to promote the 'Lift Strong' line of clothing that Elite Fitness Systems is offering. I'm going to chronicle my last week of chemo and then my rehabilitation. I'm hoping to bring more awareness of leukemia and cancer to the EliteFTS community."*

If you're interested in either reading Bob's blog or asking him a question on the Q & A, you can do so by visiting http://asp.elitefts.com/qa/training-logs.asp?tid=61&__N=Bob%20Youngs.

Bob will be missing Thanksgiving this year because he will be in the hospital, but everyone is going to visit him, and he's expecting an extra special dinner prepared by his son, Christopher. Please continue to keep Bob in your thoughts and prayers.

Love and thanks,

— Michele

It felt good to get out and see everyone. I hadn't seen a lot of Michele's family in a while. My sister-in-law, Lori, is a great person. She also has two great kids. My whole family went to the party and it was a blast. It was at one of those indoor playground type facilities, and CT was in heaven. He ran around like a crazy man with his cousin Anthony. Michele tried to get me to just sit there and watch, but I had to get out and play with the kids. I needed it and it felt great. How could I just sit there? I'd spent enough time sitting.

I think everyone was in shock to see me out there running around and jumping on the trampoline. Michele kept pestering me to sit, but there wasn't any way.

I was having too much fun. Christopher, Anthony, and I were playing tag. It was great!

It was time for round five. Cancer had won rounds one and two. I think we won rounds three and four. This would be the round to decide the fight. I was very confident going in. I had my voice back, and my butt was even starting to heal. I got checked in and got my room set up just right. I was ready.

I wanted to chronicle my last week of chemo on EliteFTS.com because Dave had started the line of clothing to raise money for LLS. I felt I could help raise awareness by sharing my experience. The "Lift Strong" line of clothing has raised a lot of money for a great cause and has really helped LLS. Thanks to Dave and Traci for helping such a noble cause.

I had to miss Thanksgiving, but I would be home for Christmas. That was a very fair trade for me. CT kept hinting at doing something special for me while I was in the hospital on Thanksgiving. No one was sharing what he had planned with me though, so I was very intrigued. But I would have to wait. It felt great to know that CT was thinking of how to do something special for me.

TUESDAY, NOVEMBER 24, 2009

Day one of last round of chemo

Dear Family and Friends,

I'll let you read from Bob's blog first and then I'll tell you what the doctor said regarding the blood abnormalities...

From Bob's blog:

> *Day one of chemo...I arrived today at Bethesda Memorial at 9:30 a.m. I was in my room by 10:30 a.m.—not bad by hospital standards. They did the usual panel of blood work. I received my first IV bag of chemo at 2:00 p.m. I'll get the next one at 2:00 a.m. so not much sleep tonight. When you're getting consolidation chemotherapy, you get chemo twice on days one, three, and five. You're off on days two and four. If all goes well, I should be released sometime Saturday morning.*

My oncologist told me they found some abnormalities in my blood cells while doing their review. She thinks it's due to some of the drugs she has me taking to aid in white blood cell formation. She isn't too worried, but she is going to do further testing to verify that the cancer isn't back. I should get the results in three days.

I've gotten pretty used to stuff like this and I just try to roll with it, but it's always in the back of your mind that you could be sick again. The chemo doesn't really make me feel worse for a couple days. I feel fine right now. Well, fine for being on round five of chemo.

I'm still tired most of the time, and my joints are killing me. For exercise, I took three walks around the whole floor. I guess the distance is about one-eighth of a mile. I don't have much stamina right now. I'm hoping to improve that once I get this last round of chemo finished.

OK, Bob is in good spirits today. Bob's doctor called me yesterday and wanted to fill me in on the blood abnormalities. She first wanted to start off by saying she was very happy that Bob's counts had recovered so quickly. His hemoglobin was at 11.1, his platelets were at 244,000, and his white cells were within normal ranges. The problem was that when they did the initial blood test, they found Bob had one percent blasts in his blood.

The definition of "blasts" is as follows:

> *Blasts: Immature blood cells. Leukemic blasts do not grow and age normally; they proliferate wildly and fail to mature.*

Bob's oncologist said that everyone has blasts in the body. Most likely, Bob's could be due to the fact that because his counts recovered so quickly, the blood cells didn't have time to mature. The Neupogen injections could possibly have caused the increase in blast cells as well. She is sending his blood off for full spectrum testing, but it could take as long as a week to get the results back (although she has expedited them).

She had originally thought to ask Bob if he wanted to go back home and wait for the results. In the off chance the tests come back positive for leukemia (which she doesn't think is the case), Bob would unfortunately need to have a reinduction of chemo again, and it would be time to consider a stem cell transplant. Bob is very positive and knows this is just an anomaly. He wants to continue with his last round of consolidation chemotherapy so that he can finally be done. I can't blame him. Six months of this is tiring for me. I can't even begin to think how hard it must be for Bob.

So now we just sit and wait for the results. The doctor, Bob, and I feel it isn't the leukemia coming back.

Please continue to keep Bob in your thoughts and prayers. I hope everyone has a happy Thanksgiving.

Love and thanks,

— Michele

The Dr. was worried about the blasts in my blood. She said we could consider postponing the last round of chemo. I asked her if it would hurt. She said it wouldn't and she really felt the test was going to come back fine. So I decided to move forward. In the back of my mind, I was worried all over again. All I could do was move forward. Would the bad news ever stop? Or the worries?

But I felt I had come too far to postpone what I was hoping was the last round in the fight against leukemia. Postponing the chemo wasn't an option for me unless it could make things worse. In my mind, the last round had started, and I didn't have time to take a time out. Can you see the finish line? I sure could.

WEDNESDAY, NOVEMBER 25, 2009

Day two of last round of chemo

Dear Family and Friends,

Today was a super busy day for me. After work, I brought food from McDonalds back to the hospital for Bob and Christopher. Did you know a double cheeseburger has 1,150 mg of sodium? I'm sure that can't be good for Bob. I read that on the side of the happy meal box. That's scary. Anyway, Bob is sore and tired. He's excited to see what surprise his son has in store for him tomorrow. I'm sleeping at my parents' house tonight in order to help with the preparations early tomorrow. With Bob and my brother-in-law's family, there will be about 25 people. That's a lot of turkey!

Here's Bob's blog:

> *Day two went without any events. No nausea yet. Not much of anything good on television. I'm starting to feel more tired than usual. I did do my three laps around the floor again. My joints are still killing me, especially my knees. My son, Christopher, came over for a visit. He made the honor roll at school and had a really good report card. I was very proud of him. We played on the computer for awhile and thumb wrestled. We finalized our plans for Saturday. We are going to sleep over my parents' house. Michele will be out of town at her cousin's wedding. I figured I should stay at my parents to make*

> *sure I'm doing OK after a week of chemo. We're planning on watching* GI Joe *the movie. Christopher is very excited to see it. Talk to you tomorrow.*
>
> *P.S. I'm really looking forward to* Sons of Anarchy *tonight. It's one of the few television shows I watch on a weekly basis.*

Please continue to keep Bob in your thoughts and prayers and have a happy Thanksgiving!

Love and thanks,

— Michele

CT made my day. We played for a long time on the computer, and he was all excited to unleash his Thanksgiving Day surprise. Neither he nor anyone else was spilling the beans on what the surprise was. He and I were both excited for Saturday. We hadn't had a sleepover in almost six months. We were both really excited to see the GI Joe *movie. I grew up on GI Joe, and Christopher really enjoys the new version.*

The fact that CT was able to make the honor roll with everything going on made me so proud of him. He was very proud of himself and rightfully so. Please understand that I have been proud of my son every day of his life. However, I'm prouder on some days more than others if you know what I mean. I only wish I could have taken him out for a celebratory milkshake.

THURSDAY, NOVEMBER 26, 2009

Happy Thanksgiving

Dear Family and Friends,

We are so thankful to have family and friends like all of you. Thank you for all the love and support you have given Bob and me. I have attached a photo of Bob's Thanksgiving surprise from his son. Bob has been extremely tired and sore all day. He doesn't want me to bring him turkey until 7:00 p.m. because he's still sleeping.

Here's his blog from today:

> *I was going to put this up last night, but I felt like crap and was very tired. I watched the UConn vs. LSU basketball game. Then I got really nauseous. It sucked. I had my fourth bag of chemo at 4:00 a.m., so I didn't get much sleep again. I was already tired to begin with and now I'm exhausted. I'm going to spend the day napping and watching football. I did get my three walks in, but it wasn't easy. My knees were really sore. I'll report more later today.*

Please continue to keep Bob in your thoughts and prayers.

Love and thanks,

— Michele

Thanksgiving was a painful day, but I had a lot to be thankful for. CT made me a really cool surprise. He used a cookie, frosting, and pretzels to make what looked like turkeys. He was so proud of himself. It was great. He came over in the morning, and I spent the rest of the day in pain watching football. I tried to sleep, but it was a struggle. I did get some turkey that Michele brought over later in the day. It was good, but it wasn't the same as eating with the whole family. Also, my mom makes the best stuffing in the world. I was really missing it on this night.

SUNDAY, NOVEMBER 29, 2009

Bob out of hospital, hopefully for good!

Dear Family and Friends,

I hope everyone had a great Thanksgiving and long weekend. I'm happy to report that Bob is finally out of the hospital as of 9:30 a.m. yesterday morning. He got home, took a shower, and spent the afternoon with his parents. Last night, he picked up Christopher. They watched *GI Joe* and had a sleepover at grandma's house. Both of them really enjoyed themselves. Today we are going over to Bob's aunt and uncle's house to recreate Thanksgiving dinner for him.

Finally, Bob should get the results of his specialized blood test tomorrow. Keep your fingers crossed, and please continue to keep him in your thoughts and prayers.

Love and thanks,

— Michele

I was really excited to have Thanksgiving. My spirits were up and down. In the back of my mind, I was very worried about the blood test. The worries were always there. I just tried to block them out. CT and I had a great time at our sleepover. We watched the GI Joe *movie twice. He was so psyched to see it.*

I think this was the first time in months that we got to relax for awhile. We were all at ease and having fun. We actually let our guard down and enjoyed ourselves. It was one more step to getting life back to normal. We spent the night laying next to each other and watching movies. I think we even had a pillow fight. He won of course.

WEDNESDAY, DECEMBER 2, 2009

Bob's blogs from the past few days

Dear Family and Friends,

Sorry I haven't written in the past few days. To make up for it, I'm attaching Bob's blog so you can see exactly how he's feeling. Hope everyone is doing well.

> *Sunday, November 29, 2009: I had a great weekend. I was still pretty tired all the time, but it was awesome. Chris and I slept over my parents' house Saturday because Michele was out of town at a wedding. We watching* GI Joe *the movie and a bunch of other cartoons. We ate like pigs and had a burping contest. It was a blast. We hung out Sunday at my parents' for most of the day and then went to my aunt and uncle's house for my Thanksgiving dinner. It was just a great weekend. I needed to stop and take a break a couple times, but I was OK overall.*
>
> *Monday, November 30, 2009: First of my follow ups with my oncologist this week. I have to go in every day for Neupogen injections all week, but I'll meet with the doctor on Monday, Wednesday, and Thursday. The Neupogen hurts like hell and makes your joints even sorer, if that's possible. I was going to start working out a bit today too, but after my office visit, I decided to wait until next week.*

The plan is to monitor my blood all week. My counts usually start to near the bottom around Thursday. They think I'll need a blood transfusion on either Thursday or Friday. Then my counts should begin to climb next week, and I can start doing some light working out. I'll keep you filled in on my progress through the week.

Tuesday, December 1, 2009: Overall, it has been an uneventful day. I received my Neupogen shot again. They hurt like heck going in. My joints are still killing me. Stairs are the worst. I did get outside and meander around a bit. The boredom of laying around is starting to get to me. I watched a couple movies and read, but I can't take much more of the captivity. The problem is my energy levels are still very low, so I can't do much more than sit anyway. Oh well.

Please continue to keep Bob in your thoughts and prayers. We are still waiting for the results of the specialized blood test. When Bob goes to see the oncologist, we're hoping she'll have the results. So far no news is good news.

Love and thanks,

— Michele

I was into my typical week after chemo routine. I had to go to the doctor's office every day for the Neupogen injections, and yes, it still hurt like hell. My joints were especially sore for some reason. This is a side effect of the Neupogen. My body was a wreck. The months of chemo and everything else I had been through had taken a horrific toll on my body. I wanted to begin some rehabilitation, but my body wasn't physically ready yet. I also wasn't mentally ready to start. I needed a break, and I think I had earned it. Could I finally let my guard down a bit? Would you?

MONDAY, DECEMBER 7, 2009

Today and this past weekend...

Dear Family and Friends,

Bob is back in the hospital for the day receiving two units of blood and one unit of platelets. He also needed additional Neupogen injections because his white count was very low.

Here are the counts as of this morning:

- White blood cell, 1.3
- Red blood cell, 2.72
- Hemoglobin, 8.0
- Platelets, 9000

Bob is in good spirits but not too happy because he has to spend the whole day in the hospital.

Here is Bob's blog from the last few days:

> *Saturday, December 5, 2009: I felt OK when I woke up. I got caught up on some laundry and other minor chores. In the afternoon, we had to go to Toys "R" Us to get some of Christopher's presents. We also ran to Office Depot and the post office. For some reason, this wiped me out. When we got home, I was tremendously tired. I spent the rest of the day on the couch and went to bed early. Bama rolled*

> *over the Gators and Texas lucked into a win. Congrats to all of the Southside Barbell members who put up PRs at the Southern States. Great job!!!*
>
> *Friday, December 4, 2009: Still feeling tired. Went to my oncologist to get my last Neupogen shot. The platelets from yesterday didn't do too much, as my counts were still very low, so I needed one unit of platelets and one unit of packed red. Again, I had to wait around for the call from the hospital because I needed those both to be irradiated. They got everything in at about 3:00 p.m., so I headed over. I got done about 6:15 p.m. I then ran to my parents' house because we were taking Christopher to see some Christmas lights. One of the parks in the area puts up a cool light show that you drive through. They even had special 3D glasses. Christopher thought they were the coolest thing ever invented.*

Please continue to keep Bob in your thoughts and prayers.

Love and thanks,

— Michele

Wow, we forgot to tell everyone that we got the results back from the special blood test and everything was good. The Dr. said this was a great sign that I was in remission, but she cautioned me not to get too excited because we still had one last bone marrow aspiration to go. Lucky me!

I can't explain how little energy I had. My body was beat up and was really struggling to get better. The tiniest bit of movement tired me out. I spent most of my time laying down and resting. I had trouble focusing mentally on anything. This is when I first heard of "chemo brain." This is a condition known to chemo patients where you simply can't concentrate or focus on anything. There have been many fine books written about it, but I had no idea until I started to research it.

Sometimes you forget that chemotherapy is the injection of poison into your body. It's a healer for the leukemia, but we forget that it also poisons the body. My body was just starting to heal from all the poison it had taken. It would take a long time to get even halfway to normal.

WEDNESDAY, DECEMBER 9, 2009

From Bob 12/6, 12/7, and 12/8

December 6, 7, and 8, 2009: I'm sure you're tired of me telling you that I feel like crap and I'm tired. So I won't. I'm going to show you my blood work. Basically, chemotherapy is poison and it "restarts" your body's production of healthy blood. The problem is there is a lull until the restart happens. This is the time when I am very immunocompromised and have little energy.

Here are the normal ranges for a healthy person's blood work:

White blood cells (WBC), 4.1–10.9
Granulocytes (Gran), 37.0–92.0%
Red blood cell (RBC), 4.20–6.30
Hemoglobin (HGB), 12.0–18.0
Platelet (PLT), 140–440

My blood work on December 7, 2009:
WBC, 1.3
Gran, 8.7%
RBC, 2.72
HGB, 8.0
PLT, 9.0

On this day, I had to get two units of packed red blood and one unit of platelets transfused, so I spent the day in the hospital getting blood.

Blood work on December 8, 2009:
WBC, 1.0
Gran, 38.9%
RBC, 3.25
HGB, 9.3
PLT, 19.0

My blood work is starting to come around. My oncologist thinks my body is starting to produce its own healthy blood slowly. I don't have to go to the doctor tomorrow. I go again on Thursday. I may even get my PICC line taken out, which I've had for about four months now. I can't wait to get it out. You can Google PICC line, but it's basically a central line that has three lines sticking out of my arm for an IV attachment. I have to shower with my arm wrapped in a plastic wrap until it's removed. I'll check in again tomorrow.

My PICC line coming out was a really big deal to me. It was a sign that the end was near. I wouldn't need any more IVs, and I could start to lead a more normal life. I couldn't take a real shower with the PICC line. I had to wrap my arm in plastic wrap and be very careful not to get any water in that area when I showered. About half of my body got cleaned. It was better than nothing, but I really wanted that thing out.

I was really looking forward to showering like a normal person. It was just one more little thing that I was looking forward to. It may seem small, but I just wanted to be able to take a shower like a normal human being. I wanted to be clean and scrub my body clear of the last six months of grime. In many ways, I was becoming whole again. The recovery process was very slow.

FRIDAY, DECEMBER 11, 2009

More from Bob 12/9, 12/10, and 12/11

December 9, 2009: Another lazy day of resting. We had family dinner and that was fun. Other than that, I pretty much just watched the idiot box.

December 10, 2009: More blood work...
WBC, 3.5
Gran, 52.4
RBC, 3.00
HGB, 8.8
PLT, 16,000

Everything went up, except my platelets. So to be on the safe side, my oncologist had me get a unit of platelets transfused. Waiting for them to arrive and then getting the transfusion took up most of my day. Luckily, I have nothing to do, so it isn't any biggie. When I was done, I went home, had a snack, and then took a nap.

December 11, 2009: Again, not much going on. I'm going to pick up Christopher from school and then go to my parents' house. I'm sure we'll end up watching iCarly *and* Scooby Doo. *Tomorrow Michele and I are going to pick up Christopher, and he is going to sleep over for the first time in over six months. It's a big day for all of us. We are going to go with Michele's family to see a laser light*

> *Christmas show. It's at the Jupiter Hammer Heads Stadium (single A baseball). They also have a bunch of other kids' activities. This will also be our first time going out to an event like this. It feels really good to be getting life back to normal.*

I think the sleepover meant more to Christopher than it did to Michele and me. This was the first time we were back to our normal routine in six months. We were all really excited. The night went great. The light show was good but very loud. CT doesn't like loud noises. They really scare him, but he hung in there. Then we went home and watched television.

For me, there isn't any better feeling in the world than being able to hug my son, say "good night," and say "I love you." That night, I slept in his bed with him. I still remember waking up and him giving me a huge hug. I can't even describe how that made me feel. I cried as he hugged me. His strength through the last six months was just awesome.

MONDAY, DECEMBER 14, 2009

The weekend and today from Bob

Weekend of December 12 and 13, 2009: It was a great weekend. Christopher slept over on Saturday night. Life felt normal again for a little while. Michele and I spent most of the afternoon finishing up Christmas shopping and buying my mom a birthday present. I was really tired afterward. The smallest bit of walking still wears me out. I'm going to start on the bike tomorrow and do some light resistance training with Thera-Bands. I'll outline my needs and goals tomorrow.

After taking a break for a couple hours, we picked up Chris and then headed to the Christmas light show with Michele's family. They had a small fair, and we played some games and did some sand art, and Christopher ate some cotton candy. The light show was OK but really loud. My son doesn't like loud noises, but he did OK. We made it through most of the show before it was time to head out. On Sunday, we woke up and Michele made us a breakfast of pancakes and bacon. Chris loves bacon. We then watched some Ben 10. *In the afternoon, we went to my parents' house to celebrate my mom's birthday. Chris, my Dad, and I watched some football. It was a great weekend.*

> *December 14, 2009: I saw my oncologist this morning at 8:00 a.m. I didn't get a copy of my blood work, but everything had improved. I do know my platelets were up to 44,000, so hopefully no more transfusions for me. I go back again on Thursday and should get my PICC line out then. I have my next bone marrow aspiration sometime next week. This should confirm that I'm cancer free and can get back to leading a normal life after I get back in shape. I'm going to spend the rest of the day laying around, reading, and watching television. I'll pick Chris up after school and then just relax after I drop him off.*

That little voice in the back of my head was speaking up again. What if the test comes back and the leukemia is back? What will I do? When you have nothing to do but sit and think, the worries in the back of your mind can be maddening. I tried to act like nothing was wrong and I think everyone bought it, but I was scared. Really scared. What if life had just been messing with me? What if this was all a tease and I was going to die? It drove me nuts. The fight wasn't over, and I wasn't ready to let my guard down completely yet. Once you get into "fight mode," it's hard to get out.

TUESDAY, DECEMBER 15, 2009

Tuesday, December 15, 2009, from Bob

Tuesday, December 15, 2009: Well, I had planned to do a little on the bike today, but my body still isn't ready. I'm hoping to get on the bike next Monday. I still get winded going up the stairs, and my heart rate and blood pressure go through the roof. So I'm going to do some Wii fit stuff tonight with Michele. It isn't much, but I need to start somewhere.

Here are the issues I'm having:

- *My resting heart rate is around 100. I need to get this down.*
- *My blood pressure is good. It's usually 120–125 over 75–80. The problem is the slightest bit of movement shoots it up. Basically, I'm in terrible shape.*
- *I am very weak. I need to start getting in some resistance training. I will most likely do that next week as well.*
- *I still have some areas in my quads that don't have full feeling back. I need to start hitting those areas with the foam roller.*

- *I have become very inflexible. I need to get some mobility and flexibility work going in the near future.*

- *My diet needs a little cleaning up, but overall, it hasn't been too bad.*

My body was still a wreck. When I took stock of where I stood, there were only two good things. My blood pressure was good, and I was alive. Everything else was terrible. Any amount of movement left me breathless and then my heart rate and blood pressure shot up. I knew my rehabilitation was going to be a long process, but I had to get through the bone marrow aspiration first. Everything else depended on that.

WEDNESDAY, DECEMBER 16, 2009

Pain management doctor's visit

Dear Family and Friends,

Bob was finally able to see his old pain management doctor now that all the chemotherapy is finished. He will be switching from the Dilaudid and Fentanyl patches (which he was able to get off last month) to Nucynta, Soma, Xodol, and Lidocaine patches. Bob has used this pain management doctor in the past and is very happy to make the switch so that he can eventually get back in shape soon.

Please continue to keep him in your thoughts and prayers and happy holidays!

Love and thanks,

— Michele

Ah yes, the pain. It didn't go away. I had seen this pain doctor before after my back surgery in 2006. The surgery helped a little bit, but it didn't relieve all my pain, so my back still causes me a lot of pain. On top of that, my joints still ached from the chemo. The doctor was very helpful and had some good ideas. It was one more step forward and I felt like I was making progress.

TUESDAY, DECEMBER 22, 2009

Blogs by Bob and a funny photo for Christmas

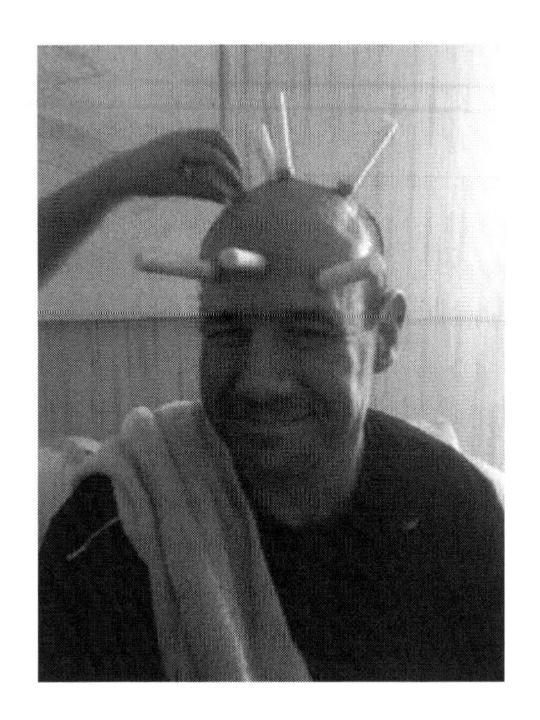

Dear Family and Friends,

Thought you might like to see a funny photo of Bob for once! This is what happens when you buy a six year old a Nerf gun.

Here are Bob's logs from the past few days:

> *Monday, December 21, 2009: I spent the day with Christopher doing guy stuff. We wrestled, shot at stuff, and ate well. Overall, I'm feeling better. I didn't do any real working out because I was running around with a six year old for two days.*
>
> *I do have a funny story. I snuck out and went to the general practitioner today because I was long overdue for my yearly physical. Mostly, I just wanted to touch base and make sure he had received my records from my*

oncologist so that we were ready to go next year. I had explained my situation and what I had gone through to the nurse weeks prior, and they wouldn't even schedule the appointment until they had received my records. So I knew the doctor had my records. He is a great guy, but he walked in and asked, "How has your health been?" Are you freaking kidding me?? I had had to get him those records and he obviously hadn't even looked at them. I said, "Great for someone who just went through chemo. You might want to look through my file." The visit ended up going well, but I was a bit upset at first.

Friday, December 18, 2009: Last night, my freaking stomach was killing me. I don't know if it was chemo related or if my stomach just hurt. I took some of my anti-nausea meds and felt a little better. I slept from 10:00 p.m. last night to 11:15 a.m. this morning. Michele was scared because I wasn't answering the phone and she was ready to send my dad over to check on me. But I'm OK. I was just really tired.

I'm going to pick up Christopher from school and then we'll workout together. Yesterday we did some push-ups, sit-ups, mountain climbers, racing, and wrestling. He kicked my butt on the mountain climbers. He does them all the time in karate class. He's excited because after the New Year, he is going to sign up for weapons class at his karate school. As if punching and kicking me wasn't enough. Not much planned for the weekend, but I'll update the log on Saturday or Sunday.

Love and thanks,

— Michele and Bob

Christopher was a great motivator for getting me to work out a little bit. It was as if he could tell I needed a kick in the butt to get going. I picked him up from school, and we came up with stuff to do. We spent about thirty minutes every day just doing stuff trying to get into shape. CT was a big help in getting me started on my way with rehabilitation. He proved to be stronger than I thought.

WEDNESDAY, DECEMBER 23, 2009

The day before the day before Christmas by Bob

> *Wednesday, December 23, 2009: Last night, I went grocery shopping for the first time in seven months. It probably seems pretty small to you, but it was a big step for me. I am starting to feel stronger every day. Today, I actually did a bunch of work around the house getting ready for Christmas. I'm a little tired, but overall I'm good. I pick up Chris in two hours and then we're going to Blockbuster to pick up some DVDs. Tonight we are just going to hang around the house. Tomorrow we have breakfast at Cracker Barrel,* Alvin and the Chipmunks: The Squeakquel, *Michele's parents' house, and then church. Then we're going back to Michele's parents' house for dinner and then to my parents' house for dessert. I'll try and get an update in, but it might not be until after Christmas. I hope everyone has a Merry Christmas and a very happy holiday season.*

Christmas was great, but I was thoroughly exhausted by the end of the day. I was so tired, I passed out. The two days had been more than I could take. My body was shot, and I had nothing left in me. I spent the day after Christmas laying on the couch and napping. I was just so tired from all the activity in the previous two days that I didn't move. I think I only ate once that entire day. Mentally and physically, I had nothing left in the tank.

TUESDAY, DECEMBER 29, 2009

Monday, December 28, 2009, the first day of training by Bob

I had my final bone marrow biopsy this morning. It hurt like heck, but I'm glad it's done. I get the results next Monday at 8:30 a.m. I spent the rest of today with Chris playing Wii Nerf and running around. We had a good day. We're going to sleep over at grandma and Pop's house tomorrow night. He is all excited. I did my first "workout" on my way back to being healthy again. I walked for twenty minutes at Walmart. I need to walk for twenty minutes, so I figured I would see if there were any post-Christmas specials that caught my eye. I left with a machete, some underwear for me, and wife beaters for Chris. I'm going to try and get my twenty-minute walk in every day and then increase it by five minutes per week over the next four weeks. Michele and I then did our lengthy strength training session of push-ups, 1 X 5 with body weight; and squats, 1 X 5 with body weight. I'll do this Monday through Saturday and increase it by a repetition each day. In the following week, the repetitions stay the same, but I'll add a set per week for four weeks. Thanks to Alwyn for sharing his rehabilitation program with me. The push-ups kicked my butt (as hard as that is for me to admit).

The first day of rehabilitation was truly demoralizing. I was so weak and my body hurt so much. I was out of breath, and my heart rate was up. I was a wreck. The walks around Walmart became a fixture for me. I had a cart to lean on and it got me out of the house. You can only sit in the house for so long. The cabin fever got worse and just about drove me insane. Imagine how it feels to be trapped in your own house.

MONDAY, JANUARY 4, 2010

Update from 1/3 by Bob

Sorry for not posting in awhile. Life has been crazy with my son on Christmas break. Well, I was supposed to start my rehabilitation program last week, but I had to push it back for a couple reasons.

My feet were killing me, and I couldn't do push-ups without being in tremendous pain. I spent most of the week walking, doing toe raises and self-massage on my feet, and just moving my toes as much as possible. I had been having trouble with the middle three toes on both feet ever since I got out of the hospital. I had reduced feeling and they hurt. The push-ups were brutal. After talking to Michele, I think the pain in my feet was caused by my position in the hospital bed. Keep in mind, I was in a coma for three weeks and couldn't move for a couple weeks after that. Well, my feet would end up just wedged in the end of the bed. Anyway, they're feeling much better.

I had my bone marrow biopsy last Monday. My hip was killing me for the majority of the week. For those who don't know what a bone marrow biopsy is, they basically stick a really big needle (16 gauge) into your hip and then scrape around until they get enough marrow to perform a sample. It really sucks.

> *I've also had my son almost every day for the past two weeks. I wouldn't trade that time for anything in the world, and we had a great time. He's very understanding when I need to stop and rest, but even with the help of Michele and my parents, Christopher still wore me out. We had an absolute blast though, and I think we both needed all that time together. It had to be difficult for him when I was in the hospital, especially when I was in a coma. He is mature well beyond his six years. He seemed to know all along that everything was going to be OK.*
>
> *I get the results from my bone marrow biopsy tomorrow. I'm really nervous. Everything in my blood work seems fine and I'm pretty sure I'm in remission, but I'm still scared as hell. Not sure I will be able to sleep tonight. I'll let you know the results tomorrow.*

My workouts got pushed off by a week. That was OK. Thank goodness I had Christopher to keep my mind occupied. All I could think about was the bone marrow biopsy results. Six months of pain and suffering came down to one test. Did I win the fight or was it just getting started? Days felt like weeks. I just wanted to know, am I sick or am I OK?

I can't really put into words how big a role anxiety plays post-chemo. I have to go to the Dr. every month for blood work. I get extreme anxiety in the days leading up to the appointment. I know I feel fine. I know I'm getting better every day, but it only takes one bad blood test to start the whole leukemia routine all over again. I'm hoping the anxiety lessens with time. My friends who have been through this say it does get easier, but the anxiety never truly goes away.

MONDAY, JANUARY 4, 2010

Bob's leukemia is in remission!!

Dear Family and Friends,

I just wanted to let you know we received news from Bob's doctor this morning. Bob's leukemia is officially in full remission! Thank you to everyone for your kind thoughts and prayers during this ordeal. It has really meant a lot. He has a long road ahead of him with regards to rehabilitation and physical therapy, but it's all downhill. I can't think of a better way to start the New Year!

Thank you again for keeping Bob in your thoughts and prayers—it has paid off!!

Love and thanks,

— Michele

The Dr. gave me the news, and I was stunned at first. Six months and I had won the fight, but I didn't know how to react. So I set up my appointment for the next month and headed out to my car. When I got to my car, the emotions hit me. I sat there and cried for half an hour. Then I sent out a big text to my family and friends letting them know the news. I went to Cracker Barrel to celebrate and have a victory breakfast.

As I sat there and ate, I thought about everything I had been through. I had no idea how I was supposed to feel. I was bluntly just numb. For six months, I had a goal to reach and I fought with everything I had to reach it, but now what should I do? For the past six months, someone had basically told me what my schedule would be. Now, I had nothing to do for a month and that was just a follow up appointment. I had won. Part of me couldn't believe it was over. But was it really over?

Little did I know my fight wasn't over; it was actually just beginning. The hard part was now starting for me. I hadn't processed many of my emotions for six months. My life had been about taking the pain of chemo and fighting. I knew nothing else. Now I had to deal with all the emotions, and for me, this would prove to be harder than chemo.

Author's note

BOB YOUNGS

WHEN MANY FRIENDS and strangers had convinced me to write this book, I had to be open and honest. I had only intended to write commentary on the blog, but the book would have been incomplete. I had more I needed to share.

The section that follows—Life in Remission—is for me and all the cancer patients out there. The second session—Lessons Learned—answers some of the questions people were asking me. Many people wanted to know what I had learned and how I view my life now. I'll do my best to share both.

Life in Remission

As I sat at Cracker Barrel eating breakfast after receiving the news that my leukemia was in remission, one question kept going through my mind—"What do I do now?" I had no idea how I was supposed to react or what I was supposed to do. There isn't any cancer manual with instructions telling you what to do. I had no idea where I was even supposed to start. I had no answers and I felt depressed. Shouldn't I have been happy? Why did I feel sad?

I had no idea how to deal with all the emotions that came pouring out. For six months, I had spent all my time in "fight mode." I tried not to get emotional. I did get emotional at times, but I had too much to deal with already so I put those emotions on the back burner. Now it was time for me to face all the emotions that had been building up for six months, but I didn't know how. So I spent the next couple of weeks crying and isolating myself.

Everyone kept telling me how good I should feel about the results, but all I could do was think about the sadness of everything I had been through. The hard part is you just want your life back. I wanted to be normal again. I didn't want to be a "cancer survivor." I just wanted to be me. I wanted life to magically go back to normal as if the last six months had never happened. Would I ever be normal again?

My body was a wreck. After six months of chemotherapy, organ failure, and infections, my body had reached its limit. I was tired all the time and I slept a lot. I also hurt all over still. If I wasn't in bed, I was laying on a couch. My scars wouldn't heal as fast as they had in the past. The wounds on my butt, neck, and stomach were still red and raw. I couldn't walk correctly, and my feet were killing me. Where was I supposed to start the healing process?

Alwyn was a huge help because he had been there before. He helped me lay out my rehabilitation program and figure out a diet that worked for me and for my lifestyle. The most important thing he did for me was provide support. Alwyn was always there when I needed him. He seemed to know when I was feeling sorry for myself because I would receive an email or phone call from him right when I needed it the most. He helped get me back on track.

I decided to start with what I could. Mostly it was just playing with Christopher. Eventually the couch and bed got stale. Actually, I think I was going insane. I was really starting to go out of my mind. So I would walk to Walmart. After awhile though, that got boring too. The problem was I was on long-term disability and eventually social security, so my income wasn't what it had been prior to cancer. Living on a limited budget means living without. I didn't have the budget to go on a vacation or something like that. I was also scared to be out in public because my immune system was still compromised. To be honest, I was afraid of everything and couldn't figure out what to do. I was going stir crazy. I thought that if I didn't find something to do soon, I was going to go insane.

I tried to express how I felt, but I wasn't very good at expressing my emotions. In other words, I just shut everyone out. I just wanted to be alone in my misery. It was as if I felt guilty for living. Maybe I should have died? No one could understand how I was feeling. My mom could relate a bit because she had been through leukemia herself, but she got it much later in life. Everyone expected me to be happy and cheery. I was mostly despondent and depressed. I wanted to run and hide, but I had nowhere to run and I didn't know what I was hiding from. No one could understand because they hadn't walked in my shoes. Everyone kept waiting for me to snap out of it. The problem was I didn't know what was wrong with me. I was snapping but in a bad way. It was a struggle to find the good in life. Everywhere I looked, I saw bad stuff happening to me. Where was the good stuff? Why couldn't I get a break? Was this my fate?

What I had was post-traumatic stress disorder (PTSD). I want to make it clear, as this term is often associated with our brave military personnel, that I am not in any way comparing my experiences or PTSD to what anyone in the military has gone through. It was hard for me to admit that I had PTSD. The Dr. told me I would as did the friends I had made along the way who had had cancer, but I didn't believe them at first. It took me several months to admit it. It makes perfect sense though. I had trauma and now I was in the post-trauma period. But I thought PTSD was only something soldiers got. I was wrong and I had to work my way through it. Actually, I'm still working my way through it. I'm still pissed off. I'm mad my life was ruined. I'm mad I have to start over. I've been mad at just about everything you can imagine. It wasn't until I decided I was ready to stop being angry that I was able to face my PTSD and admit I had a problem.

When I decided to stop being angry, I started doing research. I read several books on "chemo brain" and emotionally recovering from leukemia and cancer. I also searched the internet for more information. One important thing to remember about the internet is that there is helpful information and harmful information. There are some really great sites that help people in their recovery from leukemia. The problem is there are some people who survive leukemia and then seem to spend the rest of their lives waiting to die. So avoid the negative stuff. We all die eventually. I'm in no rush to get there and have no desire to listen to someone who is telling me I'm going to die soon. Did all the research make me better? Nope. But it did help me communicate how I was feeling with Michele so she could help. With Michele's help, I slowly started to get better.

It's been a long process. At first, I didn't want to see people or go out in public. I withdrew from life and just wanted to hide from reality. Michele made me start getting out. Christopher helped too. The two of them made me go outside and do "regular" things. It wasn't until I went out that I started to heal. Everything scared me. I remember going out to breakfast by myself. The waitress asked me what I wanted to drink and I couldn't answer. It was like life had paralyzed me. I had a similar experience at Walmart. The greeter asked me if I needed a cart. I just stared at him. You would have thought he had asked me to solve a calculus problem. The thoughts running through my mind were about infections and germs and dying because I took a cart. Every interaction I had with someone or something caused me to look at how it could make me sick again. I was literally frozen with panic by the simplest of questions. It took me many months before I felt comfortable being around people again.

I slowly started to get better, both physically and emotionally. The old saying of "time heals all wounds" proved to be true. It takes time after chemo to process all the emotions and physically heal. The problem is most people haven't been through chemo and don't understand that. They think once you're in remission, you're 100 percent healthy. They don't realize the fight is still going on. It has just changed forms. I began to go for walks and do body weight workouts. I was able to talk to people about my cancer experience without feeling resentful. I'm still healing as I write this in April 2010, but I now see daily progress and feel good about it. For the most part, the anger I used to constantly feel has gone away. I still get angry but much less frequently. It's still difficult for me to be home all day and not have much of an income. I worry that I will never be able to get a job again. How did I get here?

One of the biggest things that has helped me is finding other people my age who have gone through cancer. They can relate to what I'm feeling. Those who are ahead of me can offer me advice and guidance, and I can do the same for those behind me. I have made some very good friends from perfect strangers because they've been through cancer and were willing to help. A special thank you to Alwyn, Kim, and Jennifer. Despite their own health issues, they reached out to help me. I'm not sure where I would be without their guidance. If you know of anyone who has cancer and needs some help, please tell them to email me (bob@elitefts.com). I'd be happy to help anyone who has to go through what I've gone through.

One of my biggest issues is the stigma of cancer. Everyone who knows me knows I've had cancer. People sometimes just don't know what the hell to say. My advice is to treat people the same. I still have the same interests I had before I got cancer. I'll talk baseball, powerlifting, and politics with anyone. There isn't any need to feel different or ask different questions. People are who they are. Their beliefs may change slightly, but the true person they are doesn't change.

Meeting new people has been an issue. Do I tell them I had cancer or not? I usually just let it be unless the subject comes up. With Michele highly involved in the LLS "Woman of the Year" program, I seem to meet many people who know I've had cancer. If someone has questions, I answer them honestly. If they don't bring cancer up, I just leave it alone.

I'm trying to get back into the work force. This brings up the issue all over again of whether to say anything about cancer or not. I've decided I will bring it up because it is a part of me and who I am. It's going to come up anyway. All employers Google their potential new hires. If you Google me, it's all about cancer and powerlifting. So it is an issue that I will always have to deal with. If they decide not to hire me because of it, screw them. Cancer will always be a part of me. I spent six months afraid of cancer. I will no longer fear cancer or let it control me.

So what are my goals after cancer? My friend, Bill Lawlor, asked me this, and I have been searching for the answers. My first goal is to be a better father, son, brother, and husband. My second goal is to secure a job that will pay me what I feel I am worth. The economy is terrible, the mortgage industry is in shambles, and I'm worried that my ordeal is scaring off recruiters. My third goal is to get back to normal. From there, I'm still searching for the answers. Everyone somehow feels that facing your own mortality through cancer leads to enlightenment. In fact, the opposite is true. If anything, I have more questions about life than I did before cancer.

With all of the above being said, my goals really come down to one thing, one very simple thing—I want to be happy. How do I do this? It has been what seems like forever since I have really been happy. I still don't have the answer. I'm starting to come up with some of the things I need to do. I do know that it starts by doing a couple of very simple things. I need to get back to being me. I'm slowly starting to heal and I'm getting back to living life instead of surviving life. I'm reminded of the quote from the movie, *Shawshank Redemption*: "Get busy living or get busy dying!" Writing this book has shown me that it's time to get busy living.

Lessons Learned

People ask me all the time, "How has my life changed? What have I learned to do differently? How will I change how I live?"

These are very complex questions. My views haven't changed that much. They may be slightly different on certain things, but I'm still who I was before I was diagnosed with leukemia. I don't have any earth-shattering views to share, and no, I still don't know the secret to life. However, I do know that after an experience like cancer, you view things through different lenses when you look back on your life. You realize how short life really is and how the end might come sooner than you think.

I've slightly changed how I live my life. The biggest thing I learned is to be nice. I truly believe that the great nurses and doctors treated me as well as they did simply because I was nice to them. I've learned to look for this in people. Do you want to see how a person really treats people? Watch them in a restaurant. How do they treat the waiter or waitress who is a total stranger? Do they say please and thank you? Do they treat the stranger with kindness or disinterest? People will show you their true colors. Always treat people as you want to be treated.

Life is very fragile. I knew that before, but it was reinforced through my ordeal. You can die just as easily from cancer as you can from a car crash. My big take away from my experience—always tell the people you love that you love them when you say goodbye. It very well could be the last time you ever get to talk to them. Don't be afraid to tell the people in your life how you feel. Don't put it off until later. Life isn't a given, and we all die in the end. Make the most of the time you have here. I have one very important statistic for everyone—do you know what the mortality rate for life is? It's 100 percent. Never forget that.

The strength of my family and friends carried me through my battle with cancer. I wouldn't be here if it wasn't for Michele and my family and friends. When I needed strength, they gave it to me. When I needed help, they asked me what they could do for me. They never gave up on me and they never left me. No one can make it through life alone. Through the strength of my family and friends, I can write this today. My fight with leukemia was a group effort. Make sure you're there when your family and friends need you. There will come a day when you need them. Loyalty is a two-way street. I owe many people for saving my life. How do I ever pay that debt back?

Those who know me will tell you that I'm not the most patient person. I have little patience for mistakes, especially those that I make. I expect perfection from myself and usually from those around me. When you're in the hospital, someone else is sicker than you and needs the nurse's attention first. You have to learn to wait. Someone will get to you when they can. If you've ever stayed in a hospital, you'll learn to operate on "hospital time." This usually means the nurses or doctors will be more than an hour or two late from when they said they'd be there. I had to learn to roll with the timing of things. I learned patience through being in a hospital all the time.

The kindness of people amazed me and it still does. When I watch the news, I don't see anything but negative stories. I guess they sell better than the positive ones. I have an entire album full of 'Get Well' cards. I received more emails and texts than I could even begin to count. Total strangers reached out to me and offered help. I was lucky to be surrounded by hospital staff who cared when they didn't have to. If we could all do one act of random kindness a day, how much better would the world be? Have you done something nice today?

In life, it's important to have an activity you really enjoy, something that makes you happy. For most of my adult life, powerlifting brought me happiness. Now my body is shot, and my back won't let me lift anything. So I had to find something else. My something else was shooting. I had grown up shooting and had even been a National Rifle

Association (NRA) instructor. I'm not suggesting that everyone goes out and starts shooting or anything like that. Just find something you can really pour yourself into, something you can do and learn about through books and/or the internet. During my recovery, this really helped with the cabin fever. You need to have passion in your life. You need to live life. Discover what makes you happy and attack it with passion. Do what you love.

Small victories were one of the big themes for me throughout chemo. I firmly believe small victories apply to everyday life too. It isn't often that you score a big win every single day, but if you review your day, I bet you can find a small victory somewhere. When you feel like life is beating you down, just think about the small victories. That's what got me through chemo. Take a minute every day and think about how your day went. What small victories did you have today?

The small victories will bring a smile to your face. I think it's important to smile every day. There were times when it was very difficult for me to find something to smile about, especially during chemotherapy, but I tried every day to find a reason. It was usually from some random act of kindness or a little victory. So stop and smile. It'll make you feel better. Then again, sometimes you just need to laugh. When you feel discouraged, stop for a minute, take a deep breath, and smile. You'll be surprised at how much better you feel.

I believe one of the keys to life is to only worry about what you can control. I see people all the time get worked up over things they have no control over. This just creates negativity that you don't need. Focus on what you can change and the rest will take care of itself. If you spend your time focusing on what you can control, I guarantee you'll feel much more in control of your life.

You need to have fun. Find some ways to have fun every day. For me, it's usually playing with Christopher. He makes me smile and he makes me have fun. Don't get me wrong—as a parent, there are tough days mixed in there, but generally, we always have fun together. Remember, life is finite and we all die in the end. Make sure you take the time to enjoy your day.

The biggest lesson I learned is life isn't fair. Bad stuff happens to good people and vice versa. We don't have any control over it. I was angry for a long time about the bad stuff that had happened to me. I tried to figure out what I had done to deserve such a disease. It took me a long time to realize that crappy things happen and there aren't any explanations for it. You take the hand you're dealt and you play it. Always try and look for the positive. Life is never as bad as you think. I can't count the number of messages I got that said, "I thought my life was bad and then I read about you." I did the same thing. Remember that guy being wheeled out in the body bag? My life didn't look so bad after that.

In the end, my perspective on life hasn't changed that much. I'm still who I am. I still have the same core beliefs I had before. Most of them were just reinforced. I'm still not sure if cancer was a blessing or a curse. Every day I struggle with starting my life over again at 39 years old. I'm trying to start over and maintain a positive attitude. It isn't always easy because life isn't fair. That's OK with me though because I don't fight fair. I fight to win, and as I finish this book, I'm winning.

The Letters

A letter to myself had I died

Bob,

I know your death came far earlier than you had thought it would. Please don't worry about your son. Your friends and family will bond together and make sure he is raised properly. He will remember you because they will remind him of you often. He will know you loved him more than anything else in your life. You will always be a part of him. No one can ever take that away.

Know that your friends and family miss you and wish you could be with them again. They talk about you from time to time and it brings a smile to their faces. They remember you as a kind person who enjoyed helping others. You were a good friend, father, husband, son, and brother. You touched many people's lives and they appreciated it.

Michele will be OK without you. She will find someone who makes her happy, but a part of her will always miss you. She does think of you and she misses you. Know that your time on earth may have been short, but you enjoyed your time here. Your friends and family very much enjoyed you and they do miss you. They are moving on and trying to enjoy their lives, but you haven't been forgotten.

Rest in peace,

— Bob

Thank you to Michele

My Dearest Michele,

How do I say thank you for saving my life? What are the words? Thank you doesn't seem to do it. As we both know, I really should be dead right now. If you weren't at my side, I would be dead. You gave me life. You let me live. Thank you in a way I can't put into words.

I must admit I've been hard to live with for the last ten months. Even after I was pronounced in remission, I continued to be sick. You stuck by me through so much bad stuff. I only hope I can produce enough good for the rest of my life to repay your efforts. I truly wish I could have healed faster and made this easier on both of us.

I have tried my best to move forward with my life. It has been a long road, and you have taken the ride with me. Please know it is appreciated. I know sometimes you feel unappreciated, and I was very guilty of that. My healing has almost been worse than my sickness. Thank you for helping me mentally heal.

I learned so much about you during my battle that I never knew before. You are stronger than I ever envisioned you could be. Your resolve is unflappable. Your love is unwavering. Again, thank you doesn't seem to be enough. I simply don't have the words to express how much what you did means to me and what you mean to me today.

I love you,

— Bob

A letter to my friends and family

Please know that all of you mean so much to me. Your strength carried me through leukemia. Know that you are all a part of me. My family has made me who I am. Without all of you at my side, I wouldn't have made it.

I feel so lucky and privileged to know all of you, and it has been my pleasure to spend time with all of you. I hope I have given half as much to you as all of you have given to me.

Dave: Thank you for carrying me in so many ways. Our lives would be so different without each other. What you did for me was amazing. I will always be here for you anywhere, anytime, anything.

Alwyn: It is incredible how you reached out to both Michele and me. I look forward to the day we can meet and I can truly say thank you.

Erica (my editor) and Todd: Thank you for taking the time to make this project work and look great. Your help and friendship has been invaluable.

Bucky: Thank you for loaning me your shotgun. More importantly, thank you for just being there. You have no idea how much it means to me.

My teammates and friends from Westside Barbell, Southside Barbell, and powerlifting: Thank you all so much for your support. Know that the time we spent together will always be special to me.

My new friends who I met during my fight with cancer: Thank you for taking the time to help me. I don't know what I would have done without you, especially you, Jennifer, for sharing your struggles with me. You helped open my eyes to post-chemo life and helped me move forward.

My family: Your support was and is incredible. Know that I love you all and you mean so much to me.

The Stanek family: Thank you for accepting me for who I am and loving me anyway. Being a part of your family has been a joy. I love you all.

Aunt April and Uncle Tom: Thank you so much for being you. I hope you know I think of you as my second parents. I love you both.

Cindi: You are one of the bravest people I know. Your strength still amazes me. I couldn't ask for a better sister in the world. I love you.

Dad: You taught me how to be a man. I like to think I got the best of you. We may not have always seen eye to eye, but we always worked our way through it. Your being there every day meant so much to me. Thank you and I love you.

Mom: I don't know how you have faced all of this. You beat cancer twice and then watched it almost take your son. Your strength is reflected in your children, as they got it from you. You make me so proud, and I love you so much.

— Bob

A letter to my son

Christopher,

I could never explain how much I love you or how much you mean to me. The thought of you growing up without me was worse than dying. I fought for you, and I am alive because you mean so much to me. Please know that I have been proud to be your father every day of your life. Yes, there are times when you can be a pain in the butt, but even on those days or when you're having a bad day, I still love being your dad.

Things didn't work out between your mom and me, but I want you to know that had nothing to do with our love for you. You have a great mom, and we are both lucky to have you as a son. Both your mom and I want the same things for you. We want you to be healthy and happy.

I have tried to raise you as best I could. I hope I am able to teach you right from wrong. I hope I can teach you to be a good man. I want you to be a better man than I am. I think every father wants that.

Your strength during my chemotherapy amazed me. Every day when you walked into my room with a smile on your face, I was so incredibly proud of you. You were too young to know how close I came to dying, but I wasn't ready to leave you yet. My responsibility to raise you hadn't been fulfilled.

When I think of you, I think of us laying next to each other watching cartoons. You have a big smile on your face. You lean over and try to punch me from time to time to make sure I'm awake. I also loved being out in the woods with you or going shooting. Every minute I got to spend with you was and always will be special to me.

Should something happen to me and I die, I want you to know that I loved you more than life itself. I want you to know I am so very proud of you. I hope you will always try to do the right thing. Please always be true to yourself. Be your own man and stand by your beliefs. Know that I will always be watching over you.

I love you,

— Dad

In Closing

Dave Tate asked me, "I feel that with great adversity comes great awareness. What 'awareness' do you have now that you wish you'd had years ago?"

I had finished my first rough copy of this book when Dave sent me this question. He sent me many other suggestions, but this question sat in my mind for days as I worked on other corrections. I couldn't get it off my mind. I decided to give this question its own section. So in no order whatsoever, here are my answers to his question:

- Life truly is finite. Have you said everything you want to those you care about? I hadn't, and the result was the "Letters" section of this book. This was the hardest part of the book for me. But if I die tomorrow, I know those important to me will know how I feel about them.

- Your family needs to be your priority. That doesn't just include those who you're related to. I consider many of my friends to be a part of my family. These are the people who will be there when you need help. Trust me—we all need help from time to time.

- You should have family dinners once a week. This may be with relatives or your friends. Do I do it every week? No, but I do it probably 40 out of 52 weeks per year. On Sundays, you'll find me at my parents' house or my aunt and uncle's house for dinner. On Tuesdays, you'll find me at my in-laws' house for dinner. During that time, really be there. I don't answer my phone. I don't sit in another room away from everyone watching television. I play with Christopher and catch up with my family. When I'm at my in-laws', I spend time with my niece, Isabella, and my nephew, Anthony.

- Don't be afraid to play like a child. It's good for you. I was at the pool last week with CT, and he was jumping in and having a great time. We were at my parents' house and they have a community pool in their development. There were some other people there. We weren't bothering them or near them. CT said, "Come on and jump in, Dad! Are you scared?" I was for a minute. I was worried about what these other people would think about me jumping into a pool and acting like a six year old. Well, I got up and jumped in. I jumped in about fifty more times, and we did the craziest twists and turns that my son could come up with. We had a great time, and I felt like I was six years old again.

- The love of your children is unconditional...unless you screw it up. I've had the privilege of coaching my son in four different sports. I will say that almost every parent I've met has been very caring and loving. However, occasionally there's a parent who doesn't seem to want to be there. Please don't be that person. Being a parent is hard. It's the hardest thing I've ever done. I didn't get an instruction manual when my son was born. I've made many mistakes as a parent, but through it all, I think my son is a pretty good kid. I try hard to be a good parent. I read a lot about it, and I spend as much time as I can with my son. You chose to be a parent. With that comes a great responsibility. Embrace that responsibility and do everything you can to be the best parent in the world. Always remember that in the eyes of your child, you are the greatest parent in the world.

- The next time you see a member of our great military, say thank you. These great people protect us all at the risk of their own lives and don't get paid nearly what they should for their services. The least we can do as citizens is show them the respect they've earned and deserve.

- Embrace the kindness of others. I still remember the day vividly. My sister-in-law, Lori, had invited me out to where she works. It was January 7, 2010. I had officially been in remission for three days. I was scared to death to go out in public, but I couldn't be a lousy brother-in-law, could I? So I said, "Sure, I'll come out."

  Lori works for a military supply company called Source One Distributing (www.buysourceone.com), and the owner, Mark, and many of the other employees had been following the blog. Lori and I walked around the building and I received hugs and congratulations from so many people. Mark sat with me for thirty minutes and gave me encouragement about starting my rehabilitation. He even gave me some books, T-shirts, and hats for my Dad, CT, and me. I had never met any of these people, yet they had taken the time to follow my life in my time of hardship. Then they took the time to enjoy my remission with me. It meant so much to me, but it probably seemed small to them.

- Being afraid can be a good thing, but you have to use it correctly. I feel I'm alive due to fear. Most of you are probably thinking that I'm talking about my fear of dying. While I certainly was afraid of dying, that isn't the fear that motivated me most. The fear of leaving my son fatherless was the fear that truly motivated me. Fear can eat people up and tear them apart. When you're afraid, realize that everyone else has those feelings too. It's what you do with that fear that will define you. Find a way to use those potentially negative emotions to get motivated.

- There are times in your life when you will feel alone. Know that you're never truly alone. It just feels that way at the moment. There isn't any lonelier feeling in the world than sitting in a hospital bed at 3:00 a.m. unable to move. Was I really alone? No, I was just feeling sorry for myself. My friends and family were by my side. I just couldn't see them. They were there though.

- Anger is generally a bad emotion. There are times when you can use anger as a motivator, but usually it's just a waste of time. Michele missed a traffic light the other day and she swore as we were stuck at the light. She looked at me, and I was shaking my head and smiling. She said, "What the hell are you smiling at?" I said, "It's just a light."

She smiled and understood what I was saying. In the course of the day, we can get caught up in the moment and get mad at stuff that really doesn't matter. I've become fond of telling Michele, "It beats the alternative." My alternative was death. The traffic light and all the other little stuff in your day—is it really worth getting angry about?

- You determine what your attitude will be. Short of using a weapon, no one can make you do anything. When you wake up every day, you decide if you'll be in a good mood or a bad mood. You have a choice. You make that choice. No one else makes it for you. I've had many nurses tell me how surprisingly positive I was during my treatment. The simple fact was my attitude was my choice. Sure, there were times when I was down and depressed, but it always came down to me controlling my attitude.

- Don't be a teenager for the rest of your life. Remember when you were a teenager and no one else in the world knew anything? We all thought we knew everything back then and had all the answers. Guess what? I still don't have all the answers and you probably don't either. But through my illness, I learned to rely on people who had discovered the answers to my questions through experience. Let the people around you help and don't be afraid to ask for help.

My Eulogy

I really thought I was done with the book. I had poured my heart and soul into it. I had cried, laughed, and cried some more. I've learned a lot about myself, and I've had to face my mortality all over again. Then I received another email from Dave Tate.

Did I tell you I hated Dave when I first met him? I thought he was an asshole, but we developed a relationship and he brought out the best in me as a lifter and as a person. Now he's helping to bring out the best in me as a writer, but at times, his emails made me hate him all over again.

I was afraid to read the email. It read:

> *"Now that you've been given this second chance, what would you want your eulogy to say years from now? Once you write this one, answer what you will do from now on to make sure it reads that way."*

This email made me smile. Finally, I get to determine when I die. But when do I want to die? Think about that for a minute. When do you want to die? It's a much harder question than I first thought. I chose to die at the age of 80. Why 80? I don't want to live past the point where I become a burden to my loved ones. I don't want someone to have to change my diapers or feed me. I've been there and done that twice. But I would like to meet my grandchildren if my son decides to have children. I would like to be able to impart my wisdom on them and spoil them. I love watching my son with my dad. They work on Christopher's martial arts together after school. I hope I'm around to do that for my grandchildren.

So here's my eulogy:

> *Robert J. Youngs, Jr., passed away on a warm summer day while sleeping in his home in Florida. He is survived by his wife of 39 years, Michele L. Youngs; his son, Christopher T. Youngs; and his daughter-in-law (to be named later). He is also survived by his grandson, Thomas Christopher Youngs, and his granddaughter, Emma Elisabeth Youngs. Mr. Youngs was retired from XYZ Bank, where he served as Vice President of Lending Operations. He was a beloved friend, husband, father, and grandfather. He is now moving on to the afterlife to join all the friends and family who beat him there.*

What do you think? Sounds like a pretty good run to me. The question of how to do that isn't too hard to answer. I thought it was going to be before I started to write this. When it boils down to it, I don't need a long list. I need to do what I told my son to do if I die. I need to be my own man and be true to my beliefs. I need to love my family and friends. I need to believe in myself. I will find a good job, and I will do it well. Why? Because that is the person I am. I'm proud of who I am and what I've been through. I will be a success because I will pursue my life with passion. I hope you do too.

Afterword

MICHELE STANEK

SUNDAY, JUNE 20, 2010

Happy Father's Day to all—one year later!

Dear Family and Friends,

Today is Father's Day 2010. I can't believe the difference a year has made. A year ago today I was rushing Bob into the emergency room for internal bleeding. Now, we're spending this Father's Day surprising Bob with indoor skydiving in a wind tunnel in Orlando. It's really amazing how far he has come along. A year ago, he couldn't even wiggle his toes, and now he is walking five miles a day.

To mark the one year since Bob was hospitalized, I actually went back and read the blog (which I've never done before). Most of it was me typing frantically with a few hours sleep in a hospital on my iPhone. I was basically living on adrenaline and Bob's Aunt April's spaghetti. So I read it, not knowing Bob had added those letters to his loved ones at the end. I was balling my eyes out and he came over and said to me, "Now I want you to write the afterward..." Huh? How the heck am I supposed to follow a death letter to your son?

Reading the blog really brought back all the emotions of living those days. At the time, I never dwelled on what was happening. I was just living it. But reading it now, I'm amazed Bob survived. I can't explain how close to death he came. I think it's important to paint a clear picture of it. When I watched television or read about people having "internal bleeding," I guess I never really knew what that meant. I always figured you had a cut in some organ and then it bled into other organs and the blood hung out inside your body. (I'm a banker, not a doctor.)

After his initial round of chemotherapy, Bob started bleeding. He asked me to pull the toilet walker thing next to the bed because he had to go to the bathroom. When he was finished, I went to wipe him and I saw the blood. Bob was in enough pain so I didn't want to alarm him, but it was 4:00 a.m. and he had just crapped out "blood sludge." That's the only way to describe it. And that's how it started. For every pint of blood they gave Bob thereafter, he crapped a pint out. After six months, he had had over 125 transfusions of blood, platelets, and plasma. His liver shut down, his kidneys shut down, and he was in a coma on life support. He was on a breathing machine, and he had a stage 3 bedsore that went almost down to the bone. He had necrotizing pneumonia in his lungs, a yeast infection in his bloodstream, a C. Diff. infection, MRSA a couple times (which forced everyone to wear masks, gloves, and full gowns), lymphedema in his arms and legs, a tracheotomy that got infected, and oh, did I mention he had leukemia too?

It still amazes me that there were 125 strangers who volunteered their own blood to save Bob's life by going to the blood mobile in front of the mall, movie theater, or wherever. I can't even begin to thank those people. We actually had a scare this past month. One of the people who donated blood to Bob now has hepatitis C. When he donated to Bob, he hadn't tested positive. He tested positive many months later when he went in to donate again. The doctor said it's very unlikely that Bob contracted hepatitis C, but they tested him for it anyway. All of the blood Bob received had to be "irradiated" so even if this donor had hepatitis C then, the virus was most likely killed prior to Bob receiving the blood. Thank God Bob tested negative though. That's just one additional thing you have to worry about though. You don't realize things like that can happen.

That being said, I can't begin to express how much Father's Day means to our whole family this year. We have so much to celebrate and are truly blessed.

I hope everyone's Father's Day is just as joyous!

Love and thanks,

— Michele

TUESDAY, JUNE 22, 2010

Patient advocacy and my 'Woman of the Year' nomination

Dear Family and Friends,

As most of you know, about six months ago, Bob's doctor nominated me for Woman of the Year with the Leukemia and Lymphoma Society of Palm Beach. My fundraising just wrapped up two weeks ago. It really amazed me that she nominated me because I was such a huge pain. She said it was because of my patient advocacy. Everybody says that if it wasn't for me being such a pain in the ass, Bob would have surely died. So I think it's necessary to write something about my "patient advocacy." Like I said, I'm a banker. I don't know a damn thing about hospitals, but when the person you're hoping to marry is stuck in one on the verge of death, you learn things pretty quickly.

The first thing I did was make a promise to myself that I would do everything in my power to help Bob no matter what it took, so at the end of the day, if Bob died, I wouldn't feel guilty and think that there was something more I could have done to save him. For me, that meant putting in as much time as it took, asking questions, challenging doctors when I thought they were wrong, making hospital staff care about Bob as a person and not a body in a bed, and preaching to everyone who would listen about the importance of being proactive in Bob's care rather than reactive.

Here's what I've learned from our experience. Hopefully I can inspire others to pay it forward.

1) **Keep a notebook.** One of the best things I could've done was ask questions and take detailed notes. There were many moving parts during Bob's care. A different doctor would be on call each day, and if I didn't bring them up to speed on the events of the week, they had to rely on the scribble from the previous doctor. Bob had an oncologist, a neurologist, a pulmonologist, a gastroenterologist, a nephrologist, a surgeon, and a different nurse every twelve hours. None of them came at the same time, so it was rare that they even spoke to each other. I tried to be as organized as possible. My notebook had blood test results, doctors names, phone numbers, diagnoses, a list of symptoms, and most importantly, the names and doses of all medication that they were giving Bob. I knew that every little piece of information I had in that notebook might help at some point in the future. And it did.

2) **Don't be afraid to ask questions.** In the beginning, this was great. Everyone thought I was so prudent. It's just that I didn't know who Bob's doctor was since she was by chance the doctor on call at the hospital that day. I didn't know how good she was or if what she was doing was right. I made her tell me the whole chemotherapy regimen from start to finish, and while Bob laid there in bed, I read everything on the internet to make sure his chemotherapy was correct for the type of cancer

he had been diagnosed with and to find out what the side effects were going to be.

At one point, Bob went almost deaf. His lips had swollen up to the size of balloons, and he was twitching uncontrollably. After asking the right questions and pushing the doctors, they determined that one of the side effects of an antibiotic Bob was on could cause deafness (so they changed it). Bob also had an allergic reaction to the lip balm they were using on him while he was in a coma, which is what caused his lips to swell (so I went to the store and had the nurses use organic ChapStick). One of the side effects from a painkiller Bob was on caused tremors and twitching, so that was changed as well. Bob's not the kind of guy to speak up on things like this. He told me that the doctor's knew best. But in all of Bob's pain, I knew better. To be a good patient advocate, you can't be passive. You can't be afraid to ask questions and have the guts to challenge things that you don't instinctually feel are correct.

3) **Be proactive rather than reactive.** This was one of my biggest pet peeves. I think it stems from my job managing people. It's as simple as anticipating events such as problems, side effects, and test results and planning ahead for them. The best example I can give goes back to giving Bob blood. It didn't take a rocket scientist to know that Bob was bleeding internally and that to keep him alive, he had to be given blood. It took the hospital staff an hour to draw blood so they could type and

cross it, an hour to check to see if they had the right blood available (which was hardly ever), six to twelve hours to order the blood from Orlando, which is two and a half hours away from the hospital, and have it shipped, and three hours to irradiate the blood. Then they had to bring it up to the cancer wing and give it to Bob. There were times it took a day to get Bob blood and it really made me angry because he could have died.

So the question is how can you foresee a future event (like Bob not having enough blood) and be ready for it?

- Plan for the short and the long term.
- Work closely with and communicate with other doctors.
- Ask questions and get second opinions.
- Avoid pitfalls by preventing them in the first place.

In this instance, if the doctor/hospital were being proactive, they would've anticipated the problem, prepared for it ahead of time, and had the blood on stand-by.

4) **Humanize the patient.** I think this was one of the best things I could do for Bob. It was important to me to have photos on the wall of Bob for the staff to see while he was in a coma. I wanted to let the nurses and doctors know that "Hey, this isn't just room number 12455. This is Bob Youngs—a

> father, brother, son, fiancée, and friend. He is a person and he wants to live."

I had photos of Bob coaching Christopher's little league and photos of Christopher wearing a surgical mask. Underneath the photo, I wrote "Thank you for saving my dad's life." I had photos of us on vacation, and photos of Bob powerlifting. This really did save Bob's life. While Bob was in the coma, the surgeon came in and said something to the effect of, "I didn't want to do exploratory surgery to find out where the bleeding was coming from because I thought it was too risky, but then I saw the photo of Bob with his son and realized I had to try." I knew if the doctors and nurses got to know Bob through me or through the pictures that they would feel the need to fight for his life just as hard as I was. And guess what? It worked.

I hope this blog helps someone today. Nothing is better than being able to pass on real advice that you know works and also to say thanks to everyone who helped donate to my 'Woman of the Year' campaign. Whether you bought a "Lift Strong" T-shirt from Dave and Traci at EliteFTS.com, a raffle ticket, or a silent auction item; donated money; joined us at the Melting Pot for our "FondueRaiser," or simply just sent an email of encouragement, thank you. Thank you. Thank you!

Your kindness meant more to Bob and I than you can imagine, and I think this campaign really helped Bob's healing process. He was able to meet and share with other survivors like the Boy and Girl of the Year (a five-year-old little girl and a 17-year-old boy). It was really a fantastic experience for everyone involved.

Love and thanks,

— Michele

FRIDAY, JUNE 25, 2010

My last blog entry—hopefully for good

Dear Family and Friends,

This will be my last blog entry hopefully for good. I know it has been hard for both Bob and me to come to terms with what has happened over the last year—fearing death and celebrating life. What a rollercoaster for everyone! I remember when Bob used to write his daily log on the EliteFTS.com site. He always signed it "Be positive, Bob." I kept that with me all during his illness. In the beginning, we both saw Bob's leukemia as a horrible thing, but I believe things happen for a reason. It served a purpose. It taught us a million life lessons and helped us figure out where we were, who we are, and what we wanted to become. For instance, Bob and I got engaged during his leukemia. You might think I'm crazy, but while sometimes things happen that are seemingly unjust, looking back, I realized that without overcoming those obstacles, Bob would never have realized his true strength.

I don't believe things happen by luck or chance. They really do happen for a reason. Everything you do in life prepares you for when that something happens. All the years Bob spent powerlifting taught him the willpower to succeed. Hours upon hours at the gym taught him endurance, and his father's years as a Navy SEAL (Sea, Air, and Land) taught him discipline. All this led up to the reason why Bob survived. Bob's doctor calls Bob her "miracle patient." She said Bob would have never lived if it wasn't for the great shape he was in. My years of managing people in default service banking taught me to be proactive, ask questions, and hound the doctors to pay attention to every little detail. The perfect storm of an accumulation of both of our lives up to that point is the reason Bob is alive and well today.

Having leukemia was by far the worst thing that happened to Bob (and me too), but it has been by far one of the things I've learned the most from. Look at Bob. He met death, stared it in the face while I watched, confronted it, and kicked its ass. Bob has nothing left in life to fear, and I envy him for it. He has faced his own mortality and has come through a much, much stronger person. All Bob has left to do is live his life to the fullest.

I think Marilyn Monroe of all people said it best:

> *"I believe that everything happens for a reason. People change so that you can learn to let go, things go wrong so that you appreciate them when they're right, you believe lies so you eventually learn to trust no one but yourself, and sometimes good things fall apart so better things can fall together." — Marilyn Monroe*

Love and thanks to everyone who has shared in this journey with us,

— Michele

Made in the USA
Charleston, SC
24 March 2012